Contents

D1516739

Editorial

Koos Kingma and Caroline Sweetman

Advocacy has been defined as 'the act or process of advocating or supporting a cause or proposal' (*Merriam Webster's Collegiate Dictionary* 1995:18). To make progress towards gender equity, advocates need to devise influencing strategies which specifically target and persuade decision makers in government, multilateral institutions, and elsewhere to change policy and practice. However, advocates for change also need to persuade colleagues within their own institutions and organisations that women's rights and gender equality should underpin all development work.[1]

Advocacy to secure justice for women as a marginalised group differs qualitatively from advocacy undertaken to further a less obviously value-laden goal. The implications of this in terms of the advocacy that we do, and the way in which we do it, are discussed here by Kristy Evans in her guide to feminist advocacy. As Cohen *et al.* express it, 'Advocacy for social justice is a value-driven action. Advocacy consists of organised efforts and actions based on the reality of "what is". These organised actions seek to highlight critical issues that have been ignored and submerged, to influence public attitudes, and to enact and implement laws and public policies, so that visions of "what should be" in a just, decent society become a reality. Human rights is an overarching framework for these visions. Advocacy organisations draw their strength from and are accountable to people (their members, constituents, and/or members of affected groups). Advocacy has purposeful results: to enable social justice advocates to gain access and voice in the decision making of relevant institutions; to change the power relationships between these institutions themselves; and to result in a clear improvement in people's lives' (Cohen *et al.* 2001: 8).

Feminist advocacy and development

Women have been protesting against gender-based subordination for centuries, calling for changes to laws, customs, and social practices. This has happened across the world in very different cultural contexts – contrary to popular prejudices about the women's movement, which suggest that feminist protest has solely Western origins. Women's protests against unfair, exploitative, or cruel treatment at the hands of husbands, community leaders, monarchs, and other rulers have been documented in countries across the globe, including eighteenth-century China and early nineteenth-century India (Jayawardena 1986). Far from being Western in origin, movements towards women's emancipation have been 'acted out against a background of nationalist struggles aimed at achieving political independence, asserting a national identity, and modernizing society' (*ibid.*: 3). However, the interests that women share – 'gender' interests (Molyneux 1985) – have not been addressed in broader struggles for emancipation. After nationalist struggle ends, struggle for gender equality often begins in earnest. In her article in this collection, Khawar Mumtaz charts the development of the women's movement in Pakistan after nationalist aspirations were satisfied. She focuses her discussion on women's struggles to challenge the 1979 *Hudood* Ordinances.

Worldwide, challenges to structural gender inequality within states have made considerable progress to date, in both developing countries and post-industrialised countries. Feminist organisations and others have engaged in advocacy, aiming to promote reform of the structures of governance to ensure that key institutions uphold women's claims to resources – including not only material resources, but the law and social services – in such a way as to promote women's collective political interests (Goetz 2003; Mukhopadhyay 1998) and effect structural change: for example reform of legal systems, with the object of enabling women to live lives in which their full potential is realised. Impetus for national change has come from the various international agreements that have come out of UN events.

In 1975, International Women's Year marked the first international success of second-wave feminists in getting inequality between women and men 'on the map' as a concern for the whole world. The efforts of North American and European feminists were critical in lobbying decision makers to establish the international institutions and global events which provided a framework for organised feminist action from 1975 onwards. For the twenty years to 1995, a series of four UN Conferences on Women, together with other conferences (notably the International Conference on Population and Development in Cairo, 1994), provided an impetus to feminists worldwide to form

alliances, forge shared agendas, and attempt to shift the terms of political and economic debates about the nature of development itself. In this they were immeasurably helped by new methods of global communications. It is clear that 'the four conferences on women have generated remarkable crosscutting coalitions from all classes and socioeconomic groups from North and South, with an indisputable effect on changing awareness and programs for women in many countries' (Emmerji *et al.* 2001:103). The idea that sustainable development requires equality between women and men has been enshrined in the international policy commitments issuing from the United Nations conferences (UN 1995).

Differences among women: a challenge to political action

Yet women who are marginalised from power or resources by race, class, disability, or ill health may view gender-equality agendas as unlikely to bring about all the changes that they need in order to live full lives. However, the agendas of anti-racism, national liberation, socialism, or disability-rights movements are no more likely to yield results, since they tend to ignore the fundamental differences in the experience, interests, and needs of women and men within these groups.

The tensions inherent in social movements when attempts are made to address complex inequalities arising from multiple aspects of social identity were brought clearly to the fore during the World Conference Against Racism, held in Johannesburg in 2001. Two articles in this issue chart the experience of advocacy work to advance the interests of women whose lives are shaped equally by gender and another aspect of social identity. Therese Sands discusses the advocacy of women with disability, while Emma Bell focuses on women living with HIV and AIDS.

Therese Sands' account of advocacy for gender equality and the rights of disabled women in Australia and the Pacific charts the inadequacies in analysis and responses from both the disability-rights movement and the mainstream feminist movement. Neither has enabled women living with disabilities to have their voices heard. Sands and Bell chart the evolution of networks which advance the specific interests of (respectively) women with disability, and women living with HIV and AIDS. Advocates have to lobby to further the interests of these groups of women on two fronts: fundraising and strategising to use their resources as efficiently as possible. The mainstream women's movements should play a supportive role for those double-identity groups, if diversity and inclusion are to be taken seriously.

Diversity among women is, in turn, a challenge for feminist movements (Goetz and Baden 1998).[2] Yet, provided that commitment exists to form time-bound coalitions between equal stakeholders, based on shared goals, the challenges presented by diversity among women do not necessarily have to defeat activism. Bina Agarwal suggests that the women's movement is coming of age and recognising these truths for itself: 'among women's groups there is growing recognition of the importance of forging strategic links. One could say "romantic sisterhood" is giving way to strategic sisterhood for confronting the global crisis of economy and polity' (1995: 9).

Towards a transformational advocacy agenda

Of course, the vast majority of women worldwide need more than political or legal equality with men under the existing system of global development if their needs and demands are to be met. In 1975, it first became clear to development donor agencies that addressing women's marginalisation from development was not the real issue at stake for women from developing countries. Women from the First, Second, and Third Worlds all had radically different analyses of women's concerns, arising out of their different economic, political, and social positions. For women from developing countries, their capacity to live the fullest life possible is constrained by their comparatively weaker bargaining power as workers and carers for families in contexts in which livelihoods are constantly under threat. Southern feminists proposed solutions to these problems which profoundly challenged the politically conservative 'women-in-development' approaches of major development donors (Koczberski 1998).

Since then, a 'transnational feminist' agenda has begun to emerge, in which issues of difference and unequal power among women have been discussed and debated with some success, though not solved. Jan Jindy Pettman comments: '...with power and wealth increasingly globalised, a global response from progressive forces, including transnational feminisms, became imperative' (2004: 55). Transnational feminism has very different goals from the liberal feminism that informed early women-in-development projects. While the latter concentrated on asserting women's right to equality with men in their own nation, community, or household, transnational feminist energies are concentrated on critiquing global development itself, as founded on inequalities based on gender, race, and class (Sen and Grown 1987). In the words of Angela Miles: 'A portrait emerges of a vibrant multi-centred transnational move-ment, struggling not just for women's equality in existing structures but to redefine wealth, work, peace, democracy, leadership, sexuality, family, human rights, development, community and citizenship for a future world that welcomes diversity and honours and supports all life' (2004: 15).

Gender and development workers who sympathise with this radical critique of global development itself may struggle to see how they can work in strategic alliances with feminists to realise this vision. Studies of progress in mainstreaming gender-equality issues into development have shown that such issues have tended to be integrated into existing development discourses and analyses, rather than transforming them. Feminists working within mainstream agencies are particularly well placed to form strategic alliances with those in the women's movement, however.

Support for feminist advocacy from gender and development

A crucial part of developing a sense of 'strategic sisterhood' in advocacy for gender equality is for women's and feminist organisations in developing countries to link with development donors to work to common agendas. Development donors, with their roots in Northern contexts, are potentially powerful allies. They command funds which women's organisations often desperately need for their work; and they are able to use their location, status, and name to bring advocacy messages to the attention of global leaders. As suggested in the previous section, a mature analysis of power, inequality, and difference between women is needed, if relatively equitable and successful alliances for shared advocacy initiatives are to be pursued. A similar analysis is needed of the role that development agencies can and should play in advancing the rights of women.

The role of development donors in advocacy for women's rights and gender equality is a hotly contested topic. For the governments of the global South, the idea of donors supporting feminist activity at the national level, and promoting structural changes in laws to advance gender equality, has at best been seen as challenging, and at worst regarded as an imposition of inappropriate Western values (Moser 1989). Yet advocacy for political and civil equality is an essential (albeit insufficient) step in the empowerment of women everywhere (Afshar 1998). At national and regional levels, it is clearly most appropriate for development donors to support feminist agendas.

In her article in this collection, Rose Gawaya discusses the experience of Oxfam GB as an international NGO donor which saw its role as supporting Southern African feminist activity around the new African Women's Protocol. The Protocol has been developed by Africans for African women, legitimising the struggle for gender equality and women's rights as an African struggle, and positioning the Protocol as a 'home-made' instrument to support women to secure their rights. As a donor which itself seeks to pursue gender equality as a goal in its programme work, Oxfam saw a role for itself in supporting research conducted by African women into the potential uses of the Protocol. It has also supported awareness-raising activities among policy makers and the general public about the Protocol, and continues to support its ratification and implementation.

Advocacy for formal changes to laws and policies is, of course, the beginning of the struggle for gender equality, and not the end. International human-rights conventions constitute a basis for many national and local women's organisations nowadays to engage in advocacy and lobbying to change national laws. The success of the international lobby of women's rights activists in UN forums led to the Beijing Platform for Action – a powerful assertion of women's right to equality, development, and justice. Yet the road from international conventions to real changes in the lives of women in poverty is long, and largely uncharted. Rose Gawaya highlights the role of development policy makers and practitioners in hastening progress. The first step is to have national governments ratify the international protocols and conventions. Once this is done, the next requirement is a plan for implementation, factoring in the implications for particular contexts and populations, including systems for monitoring and evaluation of implementation, so that any problems in translating law into policy can be addressed. Hereafter, policies need to be put into practice; publicity and awareness raising is needed to inform the media and the public; and public officials need to be educated and trained. Mainstream development organisations, including donors, can play a very positive role in all these activities.

Donors who prioritise advocacy on the rights of women as a solution to the concerns of grassroots women do, however, need to ensure that their agenda does not have unintentionally negative impacts on the condition of women in poverty, or on the development of indigenous women's organisations. The article by Mary Ssonko Nabacwa draws on the author's experience of working on women's issues in Uganda. In the absence of sufficient resources to put their visions into action, women's organisations are vulnerable to having their agendas changed by donors who offer money but expect conformity to different programmes of work. Mary Ssonko Nabacwa discusses the experience of a network of women's organisations in Uganda, set up at the instigation of donors who wished to fund advocacy, as opposed to more politically conservative work with women which had, nevertheless, been informed by the realities of grassroots women's lives and local analyses of what they wanted from 'development'. Unequal power relations between donors and their 'partners' resulted in relations of patronage, dominance, and, inevitably, resistance.

The lesson here is that advocacy movements need to include the voices and experiences of the people whom the advocacy is intended to benefit. In their articles, Emma Bell and Therese Sands present examples of situations in which women realised the need to analyse their own personal experience and, from that, develop an advocacy agenda of their own. How, otherwise, can it be guaranteed that policy solutions will be appropriate? An intrinsic problem with political action in modern societies is that it usually involves spokespeople representing the interests of others; but the dangers of this can be minimised if the process of advocacy starts with a participatory process into which women can feed their concerns and discuss their preferred solutions.

New allies, new spaces, new strategies

Recently, the landscape in which advocacy takes place has undergone major upheavals and transformations, as the gradual processes of political, economic and cultural globalisation have stretched and reshaped the ways in which societies are organised, decisions are made, and resistance and protest is mounted. This changed landscape has created new arenas and opportunities for gender and development workers to pursue advocacy agendas together with women's organisations. New stakeholders, like the corporate sector, have entered the scene. Civil society, worldwide, has gained in strength, not only in quantitative terms but also in influence. As their capacity has drastically increased, civil-society actors have become more assertive in challenging power structures in an environment that is increasingly global in nature and in which the role of the State is being eroded, in contrast to that of the corporate sector.

These developments signify enormous challenges for advocacy. Whereas in the last decades of the last century the UN was a major – perhaps *the* major – target for lobbying, the era of the global UN Conferences seems to be over, and new opportunities, targets, and allies must be found for advocacy work. In her article, Shae Garwood highlights the potential of transnational advocacy networks for alliance building, while analysing two cases of advocacy situated in the global garment industry. A transnational advocacy network is a loose network of global actors which permits the creation of strategic alliances across borders. One of its current challenges is to create solidarity among garment workers all over the world. The shift of a factory from one country to another implies that some women are getting jobs at the cost of others. Shae Garwood observes in her contribution to this issue: 'loose networks or coalitions – whether part of feminist or labour movements – do have the ability to accommodate different groups of women, taking actions that are specifically relevant to their own location, while maintaining and acknowledging links with other activists dispersed around the globe'.

There seems to be promising potential in this kind of network for feminist activists to engage with other activists who are promoting the concerns of other interest groups, for example those of workers. New forms of alliance are being trialled: Shae Garwood's article describes how former targets of advocacy – corporations – are now included as allies in advocacy work. The recent wide attention given to the topic of social corporate responsibility has influenced multinational corporations, making them more willing to sit down at the negotiating table. Their interests are embedded in profit making, depending largely on cultivating a positive image among buyers. The entry of the private sector into debates about improving workers' conditions is an interesting development, and could be part of the answer to a question posed in the article by Khawar Mumtaz, also in this issue: how to engage with the 'enemy' in an advocacy strategy?

Shae Garwood's analysis also reminds us that advocating change that will benefit women is not the same thing as lobbying and campaigning for gender equality. Advocacy to improve the conditions in which women garment workers labour would have been more difficult had the campaign sought to challenge gender norms that constrain women's bargaining power in the labour market. It is far easier to pressure companies to comply with labour laws than to change society's appreciation of the value of unpaid work, and perceptions about women's economic role in society.

Conclusion: recognising the critical role of advocacy

In her article, Kristy Evans offers valuable basic advice to gender and development workers who want to 'do feminist advocacy'. Advocacy is a professional field with skills and techniques which must be learned, and feminism is a form of politics. For gender and development workers who see advocacy as an essential part of their job, it is important to get advice if this is their first foray into political action. The most fruitful way of working is for both gender specialists and advocacy professionals to be involved in jointly organising advocacy to advance women's rights in development. In addition to Kristy Evans' guide, other articles in this collection present particular lessons learned along the way. Shae Garwood points out the need to have credible and 'new' information to bring to the attention of policy makers and opinion formers. This has been a key strategy in raising awareness among different stakeholders about the impact on women and society of the phasing out of the Multi-Fibre Arrangement (discussed in her article, this issue). As advocacy is about change, the advocates should propose alternatives to the *status quo*. As Lisa VeneKlasen (2002) notes in her account of gender-budget advocacy, when proposals and examples of good budgeting are presented, the case is almost won. Rose Gawaya shows that research of a different kind is required to inform a campaign aimed at ensuring that the public knows about the potential uses of new legislation.

In conclusion, alongside the mainstream advocacy campaigns which can do much to advance the rights of particular groups of women, explicitly feminist protest and organising is on-going. In response to the end of the UN Conferences, the impact of economic globalisation on poor women, the rise of various forms of cultural and religious fundamentalism, and the 'war on terror', feminist advocates are using global communications technologies to resist challenges to civil liberties and in particular to the rights of women. The question of how to make mainstream organisations more responsive to women's interests and needs and to enable women's voices to shape development agendas remains as important today as ever.

Koos Kingma, Gender and Diversity Adviser, Novib Oxfam Netherlands

Caroline Sweetman, Editor, Gender and Development, Oxfam GB

Notes

1 *Gender and Development*, Volume 13 No. 2, focuses on the second kind of advocacy alluded to here, as part of its discussion of progress on mainstreaming gender-equality goals into the work of development organisations.

2 This awareness of difference has only relatively recently been mirrored in development agencies' increasing awareness of the impact of diversity among women on the outcome of projects which they fund (Cornwall 2001).

References

Afshar, H. (1998) *Women and Empowerment: Illustrations From the Third World*, Women's Studies at York Series, Basingstoke: Macmillan.

Agarwal, B. (1995) 'Beijing women's conference: from Mexico '75 to Beijing '95', *Mainstream*, 49: 9-10.

Cohen, D., R. de la Vega, and G. Watson (2001) *Advocacy for Social Justice: A Global Action And Reflection Guide*, Bloomfield, CT: Kumarian.

Cornwall, A. (2001) *Making a Difference? Gender and Participatory Development*, IDS Discussion Paper No.378, Brighton: Institute of Development Studies.

Emmerji, L., R. Jolly, and T. Weiss (2001) *Ahead of the Curve? UN Ideas and Global Challenges*, Bloomington: Indiana University Press.

Goetz, A-M. (2003) 'Women's political effectiveness: a conceptual framework', in A-M. Goetz and S. Hassim, *No Shortcuts to Power: African Women in Politics and Policy Making*, London: Zed.

Goetz, A-M. and S. Baden (1998) 'Who wants [sex] when you can have [gender]? Conflicting discourses on gender at Beijing', in C. Jackson and R. Pearson (eds.), *Feminist Visions of Development: Gender Analysis and Policy*, London: Routledge.

Jayawardena, J. (1986) *Feminism and Nationalism in the Third World*, London: Zed.

Koczberski, G. (1998) 'Women in development: a critical analysis', *Third World Quarterly* 19/3: 395-409.

Miles, A. (2004) 'Introduction', in L. Ricciutelli, A. Miles, and M. McFadden, *Feminist Politics, Activism and Vision*, London and New York: Zed.

Molyneux, M. (1985) 'Mobilisation without emancipation? Women's interests, the State and revolution in Nicaragua', *Feminist Studies* 11/2.

Moser, C. (1989) 'Gender planning in the Third World: meeting practical and strategic gender needs', *World Development* 17/11: 1799–1825.

Mukhopadhyay, M. (1998) 'Gender equity and equality: the agenda for good governance', *Connections* 10:16-20.

Pettman, J. J. (2004) 'Global politics and transnational feminisms', in L. Ricciutelli, A. Miles, and M. McFadden, *Feminist Politics, Activism and Vision*, London and New York: Zed.

Sen, G. and C. Grown (1987) *Development Crises and Alternative Visions: Third World Women's Perspectives*, New York: Monthly Review Press.

UN (1995) *Fourth World Conference on Women: Beijing Declaration* www.un.org/womenwatch/daw/beijing/platform/declar.htm, last checked 27 September 2005

VeneKlasen, L. with V. Miller (2002) *A New Weave of Power, People and Politics. The Action Guide for Advocacy and Citizen Participation*, Oklahoma: World Neighbours.

A guide to feminist advocacy

Kristy Evans for the Association for Women's Rights in Development (AWID)[1]

Feminist advocacy is concerned with ending injustices throughout the world by advancing women's rights. It has various uses and manifestations, from lobbying strategies at the World Trade Organisation ministerial meetings to the reform of gender-discriminatory policies. Feminist advocacy strategies can be infused with the daily work of individuals and organisations to ensure that work is maximised and targeted to changing key decision-making processes and policies that infringe on women's rights. This article describes the uses, misuses, and challenges of feminist advocacy. It offers tips and useful questions to ask, and describes strategies to be incorporated into current and future work.

Advocacy must be based on an analysis of what needs to be changed and why... this analysis must be feminist because only feminism gives an analysis of patriarchy and how it is linked to the structures and relationships of power between men and women that perpetuate violence, poverty — the crises that confront us.

Peggy Antrobus, founder of DAWN
(a leading feminist network in the global South)

2005 marks a critical year for advocacy on gender equality and women's rights. With the Beijing +10 negotiations, the G8 meeting, the Millennium Summit, and the WTO ministerial meetings occurring this year, activists for women's rights have much work to do, with processes to monitor, agendas to push, and opportunities for mobilisation. Many of the key international agreements and declarations addressing women's rights were negotiated in the 1980s and 1990s, through the UN Women's Conferences. Yet implementation of these, and hence the realisation of women's rights, has been far from universal.

New and old issues continue to surface, constantly challenging feminists to rethink strategies to ensure that women's rights are upheld, and that the issues are placed and retained at the top of international, national, and local development agendas. Because of this, there is a need for constant scrutiny and dialogue about the ways in which 'we' within the women's movement(s), and gender-equality activists, engage in these arenas. Advocacy strategies remain essential parts of the essence and evolution of feminist engagement and struggle.

This article comes from the Association for Women's Rights in Development (AWID). AWID is an international membership organisation which aims to connect, inform, and mobilise people and organisations committed to achieving gender equality, sustainable development, and women's human rights. AWID's goal is to achieve changes in policies, institutions, and individuals that will improve the lives of women and girls everywhere. It does this by facilitating on-going debates on fundamental and provocative issues, as well as by building the individual and organisational capacities of those working for women's empowerment and social justice (AWID 2005a).

AWID's involvement in advocacy has grown in recent years to include research and analysis on key issues of concern for women throughout the world, extensive communication and information-dissemination strategies, direct participation in many meetings, conferences, and strategy sessions, as well as lobbying for women's rights in key forums.

What does 'feminist' advocacy look like?

'Advocacy' is an umbrella term which describes various strategies. These include public campaigning to challenge ideas and beliefs, and inspire a critical mass of people to demand change and put pressure on policy makers and decision makers. It also includes direct lobbying of key policy makers and decision makers. Feminist advocacy, like all advocacy, draws on a range of varied skills. These include undertaking research on the situation on the ground, communicating to particular audiences, and building alliances.

Advocacy that is specifically feminist in nature is designed to advance women's rights through reforming gender-discriminatory policies, laws, corporate behaviour, and cultural practices which affect women around the world. Feminist advocacy is intimately connected to – and grounded in – the local struggles of real women, and takes its legitimacy and direction from these women, who are experiencing injustice and inequality of different kinds at first hand.

For feminist advocates, advocacy must also reflect our political commitment to realising the rights of women in the means

that we use to achieve our goals. Doing advocacy in a feminist way implies not only working towards a good end, but infusing advocacy strategies with feminist values. What this means in practice is difficult to describe. One suggestion is that feminist advocacy consists of advancing women's rights in a way which promotes four core values. These are a belief in equality; a belief in gender justice in all its different dimensions; a belief in the universal sanctity of human rights; and a commitment to flexibility in making alliances in full realisation of the fluidity of circumstances and partnerships (Sen 2003, Leipold 2001). Another suggestion is that feminist advocacy is simply synonymous with the work of all who advocate gender equality and base their daily work on feminist analysis.

Feminist advocacy is done by individuals in women's movements, but also by individuals in mainstream organisations which include a commitment to advancing women's rights alongside other complementary goals. Many development organisations have realised that grassroots development projects which address the needs of women and men at the local level can have only a limited impact on the rights of women unless the overarching political, economic, and social structures which discriminate against women, and thereby cause and maintain gender inequality and poverty, are transformed.

In order to link local grassroots realities with a feminist political analysis of women's marginalisation, feminist advocates ask questions about women's lives in a particular context and consider the links between their daily realities and the unequal power relations, expressed in policies, laws, practices, ideas, and beliefs, which constrain their choices. The kinds of question that we need to ask include *Why are service providers offering the services that they offer? What does a gender analysis of the context tell us about their appropriateness to women's lives? What impact do they have on gender relations and women's rights?* Such an analysis then places us in a position to connect the real issues affecting particular women to the policies and institutions that are producing and perpetuating inequalities. From there we can engage in feminist advocacy. The following case study gives an example of such work.

Case study 1: the Rape Crisis Centre of Cape Town

The Rape Crisis Centre of Cape Town was created in 1976 to provide counselling for individual women, and public education and awareness-raising. It aimed its services at the survivors of sexual assault, and at the broader community. Over the years, the Centre has been transformed from a predominantly reactive organisation, providing services to those affected by sexual violence, into one that attempts to solve the problem by challenging sexual violence at its source. It has built various different advocacy strategies into its daily functioning. Working with other organisations in partnership, it has been instrumental in policy creation, change, education, and awareness about gender-based violence in South Africa. The reason for this transformation was that workers at the Rape Crisis Centre realised that there were major stumbling blocks that interfered with effective service provision. Violations of women's rights impeded survivors' recovery and their subsequent participation in society.

The Rape Crisis Centre therefore established an advocacy branch, working in co-operation with other organisations branches in South Africa. The first task was to establish the issues that would become the focus of the organisation's advocacy efforts. Since then, the organisation has used numerous successful advocacy strategies, targeting different audiences and using different entry points into debates, to achieve various results. Some examples are summarised below.

- The production of a review of international and national policy documents related to violence against women, and detailed analysis of South African legislation related to violence against women. The organisation has made submissions to the South African Parliament, aiming to change legislation, and has participated in developing National Policy Guidelines for health services, the judicial system, the police, correctional services, and welfare in the treatment of survivors of sexual assault. It has also contributed to the production of a National Legal Manual on Violence Against Women.

- Identification of relevant NGOs and individuals who will provide legal support to victims of sexual offences. It has also developed close and mutually beneficial working relationships with other interested actors, including the South African Department of Justice, the Ministry of Safety and Security, the Department of Health, and the Department of Social Development.

- Participation in lobbying for changes in legal and medical procedures, to ensure that these give better services to women complainants. In addition the Centre has attempted to change public opinion, through the media, and to provide a counter-balance to biased media reporting of the issue. Activities have included writing letters to the press which highlight the extent of violence against women, and giving radio, TV, and press interviews on issues relating to sexual violence.[2]

Weaving advocacy into gender and development work

There is a misconception on the part of some people involved in gender and development work that to take up advocacy as a part of such work requires a complete shift of focus, from giving support to women at grassroots level to engaging in lobbying and campaigning activities. It is erroneously supposed that organisations should stop doing other valuable work in which they are engaged. But in fact advocacy can be effectively combined with other types of service provision and analytical work. We must ask ourselves, rather, what are the costs of *not* weaving advocacy into our work?

Violations of women's rights are often directly connected to the failures of governments to honour the international agreements that they have signed. This, in turn, resonates throughout both the creation and the implementation of local and national policies. Issues of gender equality and women's rights are intimately and pervasively affected by policy decisions taken in local, national, and global institutions. We should not overlook the strategic significance of incorporating advocacy into other activities to support women, if we want to bring about real and sustained change. Some of the most effective and pioneering development organisations have an advocacy arm (Leipold 2001). As suggested above, the critical step for gender and development workers is to incorporate a political awareness and consciousness into all their activities, moving beyond approaches which aim to ameliorate problems rather than considering how a lasting solution can be reached.

The other key thing to realise is that advocacy work can be conducted at all levels of engagement, and in organisations with varying degrees of staff capacity. Advocacy work of different kinds can take place within a variety of different types of organisation, in different locations, ranging from local government offices, national government departments and parliaments, regional inter-government bodies, international institutions, summits, conferences or events, to less obviously 'political' settings: schools, local communities, and civil-society organisations.

Navigating advocacy spaces and places

When initiating an advocacy activity, it is important to make strategic choices about where to direct your energies, and to look for strategic entry points.

Using created spaces to plan advocacy

Advocacy activities often start by using *created spaces* – that is, spaces opened up by advocates themselves, who each bring a different and independent agenda. This offers the possibility of developing a shared – and hence stronger – negotiating position (Leipold 2001). An example of a created space in which such alliances may be built is a regional meeting of specialists in a particular area of development, and specialists in advocacy itself. People who know the issues well can then weigh the options for advocacy that are available to them, and assess which option would have the greatest impact, and for whom. All the while, they would weigh up their resources in relation to the probable impact of the various advocacy activities that they might undertake.

Given the very real problem of limited resources and the urgent imperative of reaching feminist goals, it is also important for advocates to develop some sort of *criteria for engagement* that could help us to determine where we will have the greatest impact in promoting women's rights and equality, and where our efforts can, realistically, have the desired effects. It is critical to ask questions such as the following:

- Where do we have the greatest capacity and resources to effect changes in policy?

- What risks are associated with engaging in particular spaces?

- How can we ensure that our agendas are being promoted at the national, regional, and international levels?

- In what institutions are the relevant decisions being made?

- Where will my organisation, and the expertise that we have, make the greatest impact – locally, nationally, internationally?

This type of questioning allows us to make well-considered decisions. For instance, while international events and meetings receive the greatest media attention and publicise themselves very widely and effectively, it is essential for advocacy organisations to assess the potential worth of attending and participating in these events. Is it effective, for example, for representatives from your organisation to fly to Hong Kong for the WTO Ministerial[3] in December 2005, considering the cost and the impact that you are likely to have? Or would it be more effective to educate people about the impact of unfair trade on women's rights in your home countries and cities, and try to persuade them to take action? An alternative course of action would be for your organisation to lobby official representatives of your government on trade issues, in order to sway their positions, before they embark on negotiations on behalf of your country.

Advocacy in invited spaces

In some cases, you will decide that your organisation needs to participate in *invited spaces*, in order to influence the established agendas of institutions or decision makers : spaces such as government-sponsored policy consultations, stakeholder meetings with financial institutions, and local council meetings. Effective advocacy in these 'invited spaces' requires clear demands for change by skilled advocates (ActionAid *et al.* 2001:2).

A good illustration of the complexities of advocacy in an invited space is the decisions to be taken by organisations aiming to influence the outcome of the Millennium Summit negotiations in New York in September 2005.[4] This type of negotiation takes place within a very structured environment, where heads of state meet to discuss the progress towards the Millennium Development Goals (MDGs). Women's groups and organisations have limited access to this type of space, and must structure their advocacy efforts very carefully. For instance, the civil-society hearings that occurred in June 2005 were spaces where participation was by invitation only. It is questionable how effective it would be – considering their already limited time and resources – for women's organisations to send representatives to New York during the actual summit, unless they had a very well thought-out and strategic plan for their engagement in this process. There has been considerable progress over the months leading up to the summit, where civil-society groups have nominated speakers, planned strategic involvement, analysed summit documents, and petitioned policy makers. In order to participate effectively in such an event, if you or your organisation should choose to attend, it would be advisable to maximise your participation by finding out what has already been done and where the gaps are.[5]

Struggle-based issues or issue-based struggles?

There are also different types of struggle to consider. An 'issue-based struggle' is an advocacy effort designed around one specific issue or desired policy change (ActionAid *et al.* 2001: 4). In contrast, advocacy can address an issue or aim to change one policy as a single step in a longer-term struggle for social justice, referred to as a 'struggle-based issue' (*ibid.*: 5). Social change for gender equality is a slow, long-term, political process of transforming power relations. Both 'issue-based struggles' and 'struggle-based issues' can be planned so that they help to provide activists with opportunities for further advocacy efforts to change power relations and bring about gender equality and women's human rights.

Choosing an advocacy strategy

A variety of advocacy strategies can be used, either alone or in combination with each other, at different stages of particular advocacy initiatives.

Research and analysis

As suggested at the start of this article, it is imperative for feminist advocacy to be grounded in solid, up-to-date information which supports and informs a well-informed and critical analysis. You need to ensure that you have assessed existing policies and decision-making processes which have an impact on women's ability to realise their rights thoroughly and accurately. You also need to have investigated the facts about the context in which these policies were developed and decisions taken. By doing this, you can determine whether a particular policy change will contribute to the type of change that you want to bring about. Research and analysis inform decisions on the advocacy strategies that we choose, by uncovering the policy-making mechanisms on which we should focus our efforts.

Lobbying

Engaging directly with key policy makers and decision makers can be an essential part of a successful advocacy strategy. Lobbying activities are extremely focused and usually involve having direct conversations or consultations with politicians and bureaucrats. These activities can take place in various forums and with a range of people, depending on the policy and decision-making process on which you are focusing.

In deciding how to start lobbying, you need to consider the phases of the policy-making process. These start with setting an agenda for action, continue through enacting a policy, to the implementation and enforcement of it, and end by monitoring its impact. You also need to decide whether or not a particular policy change will contribute to the type of change you want to bring about. The policy process may vary, depending on the types of issue with which you are dealing. Are they relevant to a local, national, or international context? And is there a policy solution available? Not every problem can be solved by a change in policy.[6]

Alliance building

Perhaps the most important part of any successful advocacy effort is the concerted effort of movements, organisations, and individuals to reach a single shared goal. The more people involved in an advocacy initiative, the louder the demands for change and reform, and the more difficult it is to silence them. It is vital to include as many different voices as possible in advocacy. In particular, the voices of those most affected by the policy that you want to change should be included in meetings, strategy sessions, public statements, and so on.

Communication

Effective communications are essential. The mode of communication depends on the target. For example, succinct briefings and 'urgent action' letter-writing campaigns are directed at policy makers. Techniques for raising public awareness include public demonstrations, with eye-catching banners; media campaigns, using memorable slogans; informative flyers and posters; announcements via information and communications technologies (ICTS) such as e-mail and text messaging; interviews with experts in high-profile media; and various means of creative expression, such as street theatre and poetry. You need to choose the modes of communication most likely to have an impact on your target audiences. It is also important to keep in mind that there is a wide variety of new internet and communication technologies which can have a wide reach and effect for a relatively low cost and minimal effort (Evans 2005).

Building a campaign

With most advocacy efforts comes the idea of launching some sort of campaign – that is, an advocacy strategy directed at changing public opinion and mobilising this opinion to put pressure on decision makers to respond via legislation, policy formulation, or implementation. Starting or joining a national or global campaign can be a very strategic and direct way for an organisation to influence policy makers to address gender inequality, especially if the campaign is directly challenging a specific law or policy.

Popular campaigns can fulfil numerous purposes within broader advocacy goals of policy change. They can, for example, raise public awareness of an issue and spur people into taking action, attract media attention to an issue, pressure governments during negotiations, or ensure that a policy is being implemented correctly and in a timely manner. Campaigns are most effective when a particular issue is simultaneously at the forefront of policy makers' concerns and also prominent in the public mind, as a result of existing advocacy efforts that would benefit from a unified strategy in order to make specific gains (for example, the 1993 global campaign entitled 'Women's Rights are Human Rights').[7]

Effective campaigns use well-considered strategies in pursuit of specific goals. In building a campaign, it is important to identify your target audiences and adapt your messages accordingly. If you are targeting a broad audience of the general public with your communication strategy, and attempting to build alliances to engage the public in your campaign, it is important to frame your messages in a way that is meaningful to those with no prior knowledge of the issue. This is in contrast to the kinds of message that you can use to target policy makers who already know about the issue, whose support you are hoping to attract, and in contrast also to messages designed to change the minds of policy makers who are opposed to the changes that you are advocating. You need to structure your strategies and messages in ways that will maximise the impact on your audiences. Select strategies that are appropriate for the issues at hand, and to the goal of achieving sustainable social transformation.

Always remember to consult like-minded organisations (especially locally based organisations) about the most appropriate and effective strategy for your campaign.

These are some questions to ask when designing or joining a campaign:

- Why is my organisation joining/creating this campaign? What outcomes are we hoping for?

- Who/what is this campaign supporting?

- Who is supporting the campaign, and why?

- Is this campaign supported at different levels?

- Is it grounded in the daily struggles of people whose lives could be improved by a successful achievement of the campaign's goal?

- Is this campaign linked to a strategic moment or a particular political venue that is appropriate to the issue?

- Will the campaign raise public awareness and encourage citizen participation in decision making?

- Will the campaign contribute to the transformation of power relations?

The next case study provides an example of a campaign which is viewed by many as a campaign 'gone wrong', owing to a failure to consider such issues.

*Case study 2: the Amina Lawal
letter-writing campaign*

Many readers may remember being bombarded by e-mails in 2002 which pleaded with members of the public to join an international letter-writing campaign to save the life of Amina Lawal, a young Nigerian woman who was sentenced to stoning to death for alleged adultery in August that year.[8] According to the campaign, her life was in imminent danger. However, the campaign letter that was being circulated for signing contained inaccurate information and perpetuated negative misconceptions about Islam and Muslims. A Nigerian women's rights group, Baobab, was familiar with, and sensitive to, the local situation and the particular details of the case. According to Baobab, the campaign's letter-writing strategy was not appropriate in this situation, because of the volatility of the local context. They were concerned that the campaign might aggravate the situation and put Amina Lawal and her supporters in danger from vigilantes.
(See www.whrnet.org/docs/action-03-05-07.html, last checked 2 September 2005.)

This case study offers several lessons for advocates to keep in mind. First, get your facts right. Second, find out which local activists and organisations are already engaged in working on the issue, and consult them. Third, revise your plans in partnership with those who are directly involved.

Has our advocacy work been effective? How will I know?

To measure the success of your advocacy efforts, it is essential to have clearly identified the goals of your advocacy strategy in advance. From this you can then measure your outcomes. Critical questions to ask when designing advocacy initiatives include the following:

- What is the focus of our advocacy strategy?
- Who are our target audiences, and what do we want to achieve through them?
- What is the impact that we hope to achieve through these strategies?
- What are the actual policy-change and decision-making structures that we want to change/influence?

Incorporating these questions into the initial design of your advocacy efforts will not only allow careful consideration of *what* exactly you are trying to achieve, but will help you to plan *how* you will achieve your goals. In this way, you can measure your successes by the impact that your advocacy strategies have had, and you can learn from your experiences.

This approach also prompts you to ask, when assessing how you will achieve the advocacy goals, where the resources will be obtained for the advocacy strategy.[9]

Alliance building as an engine for change

Feminist advocacy can (and should) be used on the ground and in local struggles. But it can also very effectively link the global and global dimensions, by challenging the effects on women in a particular context of national and international policies and decisions.

One way of doing this is to promote the participation of grassroots groups themselves in advocacy. For instance, if a community is fighting against the privatisation of water supplies, and associated cost-recovery programmes, feminist advocacy enables communities to plan their response by using a political analysis of the impact of the policy on women, men, and children. It can also provide them with conceptual tools which help them to identify strategic opportunities to enter debates and processes, and target audiences for their messages.

Feminist advocacy initiatives can also link regional struggles with international struggles. They can provide a concrete plan of action for activists from different regions to consolidate their efforts. A good example of this is the GCAP-women's list, which is a communication mechanism that enables interested women's organisations and groups to strategise, disseminate information, and ensure that women's-rights perspectives are being included in the major negotiations both at the regional and global levels.[10]

This kind of alliance building enables a range of organisations from regions throughout the world to consolidate their advocacy efforts, and thereby achieve more impact. Feminist advocacy can also involve women's organisations working together with allies from mainstream development and other sectors to address issues such as trade liberalisation, food security, peace building, violence against women, and migration. Advocates from different regions and sectors can consolidate their efforts and resources in a thoughtful and strategic way, assessing goals and ensuring that advocacy strategies are used in the most effective ways possible.

Conclusion

Currently, very significant challenges remain for advocates of women's rights.[11] There is a concern that the intense advocacy efforts of 2005 have been expended on defending goals that had already been negotiated and 'won' in previous forums. This has left little time and few resources for developing and promoting a proactive agenda in support of women's rights. Shrinking resources and funding for work on women's rights are another source of serious concern. AWID's recent survey, entitled 'Where is the Money for Women's Rights?', has shown that advocacy activities are difficult to fund. Increasingly, the resources of international development agencies that used to fund NGOs are now going directly to governments. This is potentially problematic for advocacy initiatives that criticise government policies.

As advocates for women's rights, we need to be mindful of how we work with allies, with the media, and among ourselves to ensure the greatest possible impact. Alliance building is a critical part of advocacy efforts, but advocates for women's rights still feel that gender equality, recognised to be critical to poverty alleviation and the elimination of injustices throughout the world, is still marginalised by many mainstream international advocacy organisations and omitted from their advocacy agendas. Another problem is the lack of capacity within the women's movement to link different advocacy issues. An example of this is the polarisation of issues relating to economic justice and sexual rights in the women's movement. Although these issues are fundamentally interconnected, they are often treated as single issues, to be pursued with single-minded strategies. A final challenge for advocates of women's rights is that strong and influential advocacy depends heavily on engaging the interest of the media, which unfortunately still promote misconceptions about feminists and portray women as 'victims'.

It is critical to secure a feminist presence in key negotiation processes, to ensure that women's rights are positively and not negatively affected. This entails work for advocates of women's rights in both mainstream development organisations and women's organisations and groups. We must focus on including women's and feminist voices not only at the actual negotiations, but also in the processes leading up to them. We must create opportunities to develop strategies of our own that integrate issues, build alliances, and implement our advocacy measures as effectively as possible. We must ensure that the public is educated by means of popular campaigning and mobilisation around the issues; that national-level representatives promote a women's rights agenda; and that we, as advocates, are taking up and using our opportunities at the 'invited spaces'. It is via creative, careful, and well-thought strategies that we shall realise women's rights.

Kristy Evans is currently completing her Master's degree in Public Health at the University of Cape Town, and acts as a part-time consultant in the fields of gender, human rights, and development. She has worked with AWID for the past four years in various capacities. Postal address: 31 St. Joan's Rd, Plumstead, Cape Town, 7800, South Africa. Email: kevans@awid.org

Notes

1 I thank Alison Symington for her initial editing of this paper.
2 See www.rapecrisis.org.za/ for more information.
3 The WTO Ministerial is the highest-level decision-making body of the World Trade Organisation (WTO), meeting approximately every two years and setting the agenda of the organisation. At the Hong Kong Ministerial, delegates are attempting to get negotiations back on track to implement the 'Doha Agenda' (as articulated at the fourth Ministerial in Doha, Qatar, November 2001) (AWID 2005b). More information about the Hong Kong WTO Ministerial is available at www.awid.org/go.php?pg=year_ opportunities.
4 To find out more about the Millennium +5 Summit, visit www.awid.org/go.php?pg=year_ opportunities.
5 To find out what women's organisations have done in relation to the Millennium +5 Summit, consult the GCAP-women's list archives at http://mailman-new.greennet.org.uk/pipermail/gcap-women/.
6 Sisonke Msimang, personal interview, November 2003.
7 'Women's Rights are Human Rights' was a global campaign organised to coincide with the 1993 World Conference on Human Rights in order to ensure that women's rights were taken seriously and placed on the agenda for negotiation (CWGL 2005).
8 The UK chapter of Amnesty International started a petition which attracted 1.3 million signatures in support of Amina (Break the Chain, 2005)
9 More information on resources for the women's movement can be obtained in a forthcoming report by The Association for Women's Rights in Development (AWID), which will be found at www.awid.org. This was based on a survey called 'Where is the Money for Women's Rights?', conducted in 2005 with members of AWID.
10 To see the GCAP-women's list archives, go to http://mailman-new.greennet.org.uk/pipermail/gcap-women/.
11 The challenges for women's rights advocates have been highlighted in conversations with staff at AWID staff, especially Joanna Kerr.

References

ActionAid, Institute for Development Studies Participation Group, and Just Associates (2001) 'Making Change Happen: Advocacy and Citizen Participation', www.justassociates.org/MakingChange Report.pdf. Last checked on 2 September 2005.

AWID (2005a) 'About AWID', www.awid.org/go.php?pg=about. Last checked 1 September 2005.

AWID (2005b) 'The World Trade Organization 6th Ministerial Conference, Hong Kong, December 13-18, 2005', www.awid.org/go.php?pg=year_opportunities. Last checked 2 September 2005.

Break the Chain (2005) 'Save Amina', www.breakthechain.org/exclusives/amina.html. Last checked 2 September 2005.

Center for Women's Global Leadership (CWGL) (2005) 'Policy and advocacy program', www.cwgl.rutgers.edu/globalcenter/policy/policy.html. Last checked 2 September 2005.

Evans, K. (forthcoming 2005) 'Cyber girls: hello...are you out there?' in S. Wilson, A. Sengupta, and K. Evans (eds.) *Defending our Dreams: Global Feminist Voices for a New Generation*, London: Zed Books.

Leipold, G. (2001) 'Campaigning: a fashion or the best way to change the global agenda?', in D. Eade and E. Ligteringen (eds.) *Debating Development*, Oxford: Oxfam GB.

Sen, G. (2003) 'Lecture notes' from the DAWN Advocacy Institute in Bangalore, India.

Politics at work:
transnational advocacy networks and the global garment industry

Shae Garwood

In the past two decades, hundreds of thousands of women and girls, from El Salvador to Lesotho, have earned their livelihoods by sewing clothes for the global garment industry. With the phasing out of the Multifibre Arrangement (MFA) at the end of 2004, many of these women face the prospect of unemployment. The use of transnational advocacy networks in two campaigns, the MFA Forum and Play Fair At The Olympics, may provide some lessons for gender and development advocates concerned about the fate of the millions of women working on the global assembly line.

The garment industry is undergoing dramatic changes in response to the phasing out of the Multifibre Arrangement (MFA) at the end of 2004. This could mean massive job losses for some of the 29.3 million people working in the textile, clothing, and footwear industry worldwide, many of whom are women (International Labour Organization 2000: 13). These changes illustrate the need for transnational advocacy as factories close, women are left unemployed, and countries compete in what some have called a 'race to the bottom'.

North American and European governments first implemented the MFA in 1974 to protect their own textile manufacturers. The MFA prescribed an elaborate quota system which limited the quantity of clothing and textiles that each country could export to the United States, Canada, and Europe. Since quotas limited the amount that could be produced in any one country, the garment industry spread out over nearly 200 countries. An unintended consequence of North American and European protectionism was that the garment industry became an important part of many local economies in the South, providing much-needed revenue and jobs in countries that would not have otherwise developed a competitive garment sector. Although the wages and working conditions of these jobs were often poor, they did provide income for workers who had few alternatives.

For example, in Lesotho, the garment and textile industry accounts for 99 per cent of the country's export earnings (Kearney 2005). Many factories in Lesotho had shut down by mid-2005, leaving workers with few employment alternatives. Lesotho Haps and Vogue Landmark, two of the largest factories that produced goods for Walmart, recently shut their doors, leaving 2,000 employees out of work (Iritani and Dickerson 2005). Meanwhile in El Salvador, business leaders are trying to avoid factory closures and stay ahead of the competition by reducing the already abysmal minimum wage of $5.04 a day (Marshall *et al.* 2005).

Although women in many countries will suffer with the end of the quota system, several national economies, mainly China and India, stand to gain. In the first few months of 2005, Chinese clothing exports to the USA increased 75 per cent from the previous year (Brooke 2005). This caused an outcry from many American and European manufacturers and government officials. The US government recently reinstated a quota on some Chinese goods, and the EU recently filed a complaint with the WTO, aiming to limit exports of Chinese T-shirts and flax yarn (Goodman 2005). Despite the increased production of Chinese goods, there is no guarantee that working conditions for Chinese workers will improve. In fact, it is more likely that working conditions will actually decline as competition increases among developing countries, resulting in an increasingly downward pressure on wages (Chan 2003; Foo and Bas 2003).

One way to address these issues is by linking garment workers' struggles around the world through what Keck and Sikkink (1998) refer to as *transnational advocacy networks*. These are 'organised to promote causes, principled ideas, and norms, and they often involve individuals advocating policy changes that cannot be easily linked to a rationalist understanding of their "interests"' (*ibid.*: 8). These networks may consist of a variety of actors: NGOs, foundations, elements of the media, churches, trade unions, and parts of inter-government organisations or governments, depending on the particular issue.

The garment industry presents one of the clearest examples of the differential impacts of trade policies and practices on women and men. Women are employed in far greater numbers than men in the garment industry, and often occupy lower-paid positions. Employers often hire young women, for reasons that include assumptions about women's supposedly 'inherent' skills, their patience in dealing with repetitive tasks, and their reluctance to demand better working conditions and higher wages (Elson and Pearson 1981). Gender discrimination and inequality have proved to be extraordinarily profitable for businesses. Multinational corporations rely on the competitive advantage of women's disadvantage locally, to suppress wages across the industry globally. Transnational advocacy networks are an appropriate response, since – in the absence of cross-border organising – employers will continue to take advantage of, and even exacerbate, gender inequalities in order to minimise costs and maintain a competitive edge.

The ultimate effects of transnational advocacy efforts related to the MFA remain to be seen, but past campaigns and strategies may provide some lessons for gender and development practitioners and activists concerned about the fate of the millions of women who earn their livelihoods in the global garment industry.

As a researcher and activist based in Australia, I am not at risk of losing my income as a result of the whims of Walmart executives and subcontractors, or backroom deals among trade ministers. However, we are all inextricably linked through the global trading system. The products that we make, buy, or sell (or refuse to make, buy, or sell, for that matter) have the power to reinforce inequalities and exploitation, or facilitate development in a way that respects workers' rights and human dignity.

The next section considers two important challenges facing transnational advocacy networks: working with difference, and gaining access to inter-government bodies. After this I examine two case studies, the MFA Forum and Play Fair At The Olympics, which employed very different strategies to address exploitation and the negative effects of the global garment industry. The article concludes with some thoughts on the gendered implications of each case study, and reflections on how transnational advocacy networks can begin to address some of the difficult issues facing workers, activists, and gender and development practitioners.

Problems faced by transnational advocacy networks

Working with difference

Despite the potential for transnational advocacy networks to create strategic alliances across borders, significant difficulties are encountered in actually getting these alliances to work smoothly, especially in cases where workers have been pitted against each other – and where gains made in one location may mean very real losses for workers elsewhere. Corporations benefit greatly from the current structure of the garment industry, which fosters intense competition among developing countries to attract foreign investment. Many factories are located in export-processing zones in order to take advantage of 'tax holidays' and other favourable conditions provided by host governments. Organised workers are aware that speaking up and demanding their rights may actually encourage corporations to relocate to other places where workers are less vocal (Merk 2005c). In other words, workers have very little room to manoeuvre, because of the absence of adequate legislation and/or a failure to enforce existing labour laws.

This has been an on-going struggle for global labour movements. While projects such as the Southern Initiative on Globalisation and Trade Union Rights have made gains in recent years, there are no easy ways to build solidarity among the world's garment workers. This remains one of the most pressing labour issues of our time, and regrettably this article can only raise the issue, rather than resolve it.

However, lessons can be drawn from feminists who have faced similar challenges in global women's movements. Many women have rejected calls for global sisterhood, pointing out that the notion of sisterhood ignores the complexities of difference and local situations. Although they can be very difficult to form and operate, loose networks or coalitions – whether part of feminist or labour movements – do have the ability to accommodate different groups of women, taking actions that are specifically relevant to their own location, while maintaining and acknowledging links with other activists dispersed around the globe.[1] The challenge faced by activists, regardless of their own location in the global economy, is to create cross-border relationships and networks which avoid pitting poor women against each other as regional opponents in the global labour market, and which honour the depth and complexity of individual difference.

One way to do this is for networks to raise awareness among women workers of their shared identities as women workers in an interconnected global labour market. Applying the concept of transnational advocacy networks to the garment industry does not imply that all women (or men) working in the garment industry face the same circumstances, or that their desires or needs overlap; but it does acknowledge that there may be common issues around which they can organise. Without co-operation among garment workers around the world, the only guaranteed 'winners' will be the multinational corporations that are able to capitalise on increasing competition among workers for limited jobs.

Gaining access to inter-government bodies

Another challenge for transnational advocacy networks is to secure meaningful access to inter-government bodies such as the World Trade Organisation (WTO). The WTO pays lip service to NGO involvement; however, its website makes clear that while many of the organisations with whom it consults may, technically, have non-government or non-profit status, many of them serve the business interests of the multinational corporations. For example, among the 'NGOs' that recently submitted briefings to the WTO, the International Chamber of Commerce, the National Foreign Trade Council, and International Financial Services were included. The inaccessibility and undemocratic nature of the WTO may have contributed to the decision of MFA Forum and Play Fair organisers to employ other channels to advocate improved conditions for garment workers.

Case study 1: the MFA Forum

As described above, the phasing out of the MFA has had a dramatic impact on the global garment industry, with more factories expected to close in the near future. The MFA itself actually ended in 1994, but the Agreement on Textile and Clothing extended quotas on textile and clothing exports to Northern markets until 1 January 2005. The purpose of the Agreement on Textile and Clothing was to remove the quotas gradually over a ten-year period to ease the transition. However, Northern governments – whose tax bases benefited from the protectionism – found ways to delay the gradual phase-out. They left 80 per cent of the quotas intact until the end of 2004, causing a huge shock to factory workers worldwide when the phase-out finally ended.

In March 2004, a group of more than 30 multilateral institutions, NGOs, and businesses came together through the MFA Forum to analyse the potential impact of the phase-out of the quota system and develop collaborative, co-ordinated actions to address the needs of displaced workers and affected communities.[2] What makes this group unique is that it includes NGOs, trade unions, and inter-government organisations, as well as several corporations. The aims of the Forum are to 'further the understanding of the likely impacts on apparel-manufacturing countries of the phase-out of the MFA, and to identify possible courses of action to mitigate the social consequences of this, based on respect for international labour rights' (MFA Forum 2005a).

The MFA Forum recently published 'A Collaborative Framework for Guiding Post-MFA Actions'. This document includes recommendations for trade unions, NGOs, clothing manufacturers, buyers, exporting countries, importing countries, and inter-government organisations: recommendations that range from up-grading technologies in order to maintain competitiveness to providing retraining programmes for displaced workers (MFA Forum 2005b). MFA Forum members agreed that 'engagement at a country level should be done on the basis of ensuring efforts are or lead to "home owned" and "home grown" actions' (MFA Forum 2005a). Local control is certainly an important aspect of efforts to create lasting solutions; however, by focusing on local solutions, organisers risk misrepresenting the systemic and global nature of exploitation in the garment industry and underestimating the need for industry-wide solutions.

Contributing a private-sector perspective on the MFA, corporate executives claimed that they have few, if any, obligations to workers (Business for Social Responsibility 2004). Instead, the executives argued that governments, local industry associations, and the factories themselves were responsible for affected workers and their communities. This is a good example of how the structure of the garment industry works to distance multinational corporations from suppliers, allowing them to avoid any responsibilities for the conditions under which the goods that they purchase are produced. One executive commented,

'Companies have already been serving as "police", monitoring factories and doing the governments [sic] job, we certainly can't also be expected to play a "welfare role"'(*ibid.*,16). While the claim that companies actually take an active role in monitoring factories for compliance is debatable, it is clear that this executive felt that the well-being of displaced or mistreated workers was not his company's responsibility.

One of the main achievements of the MFA Forum so far is its work with the United Nations Development Programme (UNDP), aiming to ensure that Bangladesh maintains its textile and garment industry. Following a UNDP / MFA Forum conference in Dhaka in June 2005, the Bangladeshi government expanded the National Forum on Social Compliance to promote compliance with international labour standards (ETI 2005). While this initiative is a positive sign for workers, it is based on the assumption that Bangladesh's garment industry will remain attractive to transnational corporations and buyers. However, as working conditions improve, labour costs are likely to rise, which could lead manufacturers to relocate to lower-cost regions. Buyers certainly take other factors into consideration – such as quality, transportation time to market, and flexibility – but cost is still the primary determinant in locating production.

While the focus of the MFA / UNDP initiative on increasing compliance with labour laws in Bangladesh is important for Bangladeshi workers, it assumes that multinational corporations would be likely to stay in Bangladesh – and pay more for goods – rather than take advantage of cheaper production elsewhere. But if corporations viewed adherence to labour laws as a competitive advantage (and were willing to pay the associated costs), they would most likely not have set up factories in Bangladesh in the first place. According to the Forum (MFA 2005a), 'By using the framework developed by The Forum, it is hoped that Bangladesh, as well as other

countries where the MFAF will be engaging, can develop a strategy of responsible competition which would address the rights of workers in the restructuring of the global garment industry as well as addressing issues of trade.' This puts the burden on Southern governments to develop strategies that will entice garment manufacturers to remain where they are – and possibly further subsidise the industry – rather than putting the onus on the industry as a whole to take responsibility for the well-being of the women and men who work on the factory floors.

The MFA Forum is establishing a project in Lesotho, and the World Bank recently adopted the MFA Forum Collaborative Framework for its work in Cambodia. While these initiatives are a step in the right direction, it is not yet clear whether other members of the public and private sectors will adopt and implement the recommendations, or what effect those actions will have on garment workers worldwide.

Case study 2: Play Fair At The Olympics

The Clean Clothes Campaign (CCC), eleven Oxfam affiliates, and Global Unions designed the 'Play Fair At The Olympics' campaign to draw attention to the exploitation of workers in the sportswear industry. Campaign organisers timed the campaign to coincide with the 2004 Olympic Games, held in Athens.[3] Although campaign organisers did not create the campaign specifically to address the phase-out of the MFA, the campaign focused on working conditions, compliance, and fair labour practices in the sportswear industry, which is a sub-set of the garment sector affected by the MFA.

The campaign included 500 demonstrations, protests, and picket lines in more than 35 countries. One such activity included activists and athletes carrying an alternative torch through major garment-producing centres in India (Murthy 2004).

All of the activities around the world focused on raising awareness among members of the public, and generating public pressure on the sportswear industry. The campaign focused on the International Olympic Committee and seven brands: Asics, Fila, Kappa, Lotto, Mizuno, Puma, and Umbro. Until the Campaign began, the seven brands had escaped the level of scrutiny that the major three (Nike, Reebok, and Adidas) had faced (Merk 2005a: 6). By focusing on these companies, along with earlier actions aimed at the three top retailers, the Play Fair campaign aimed to create industry-wide change. This approach is particularly appropriate, because many of the factories and suppliers in question produce goods for multiple brands.

In addition to the petitions, street protests, and other direct actions, the campaign engaged with the companies through letters and meetings. Campaign organisers issued a report entitled *Play Fair At The Olympics* and convened a sectoral meeting at the International Labour Organization. The report contained extensive research from six countries, highlighting the results of 186 interviews with workers and 10 representatives of sportswear companies. It documented extensive violations in factories that produce goods for each of the targeted brands.

The companies' responses to the campaign varied. Some even acknowledged the need to develop an industry-wide approach to labour abuses through the World Federation of Sporting Goods Industries (WFSGI), although neither the WFSGI nor the International Olympic Committee was particularly responsive to the demands of the Play Fair organisers. In fact, although representatives of the WFSGI did meet with Play Fair organisers, they told them that the WFSGI was unwilling and unable to co-ordinate a sector-wide approach to labour abuses in the industry (Miller 2005).

A major focus of the campaign was the freedom of assembly of trade unions and labour-rights groups. Puma, Umbro, Asics, and Mizuno made commitments to improve their labour policies. Fila, Lotto, and Kappa were less co-operative. Asics joined the Fair Labor Association, but it is unclear whether Umbro will follow suit (Merk 2005d). While the results varied among companies, the campaign as a whole successfully raised awareness, pressured the companies to be more accountable, and made it clear that their labour practices were under greater scrutiny by the international community. However, the Campaign's direct impact on working conditions is still unclear.

Several other campaigns in recent years have used similar advocacy efforts to target corporations, with varying degrees of success. They include campaigns aimed at Nike, Nestlé, and The Gap. According to Jeroen Merk, Research Coordinator at the International Secretariat of CCC, Play Fair 'was one of the first campaigns that pursued a singular, unified strategy' (Merk 2005b). This is in contrast, for example, to NGOs' and unions' pursuit of differing strategies in the Nike campaigns, which often led to confusion for organisers as well as frustration from targeted companies (Connor 2004). In addition to its focus on industry-wide solutions, the Play Fair campaign represents an increasingly important trend in transnational labour advocacy: collaboration between NGOs and trade unions. In fact, building relationships among the campaign organisers was a significant achievement of the campaign, which will encourage greater co-operation in the future (Merk 2005c). For example, the campaign organisers developed a Programme of Work with clear guidelines and goals for the sportswear industry that can be used in future campaigns.

Politics at work: lessons learned

At first glance it may appear that there are few similarities between the MFA Forum and the Play Fair campaign. However, they both provide lessons about transnational advocacy networks – their strengths, weaknesses, and opportunities for the future, particularly as they relate to women working in the garment industry. An effective way to begin to understand the factors that contribute to, or limit, the success of transnational advocacy networks is to examine what Keck and Sikkink (1998:16) call the typology of tactics – or politics – used by campaigns. These tactics include *information politics, symbolic politics, leverage politics,* and *accountability politics,* each of which is discussed below.

Information politics

Keck and Sikkink *(op. cit.*: 16) define information politics as the 'ability to quickly and credibly generate politically usable information and move it to where it will have the most impact'. Both the MFA Forum and Play Fair organisers relied on credible information to gain support for their position, particularly information that was not being presented in the mainstream media or by 'official' sources. The presentation of information, particularly research-based findings, was a key strategy employed in both cases. The Play Fair campaign produced an extensive report, which included testimonials from workers, with extensive data to document abuses and also personalise the findings of the research. The MFA Forum presented significant data in their report, *Mapping the End of the MFA* (Accountability 2005). This document drew upon existing research and focused particular attention on ten countries where the outcome of the end of the MFA is uncertain, and where the garment industry plays a significant role in the domestic economy.

With this critical information, the networks attempted to gain credibility with their target audiences. The targets of Play Fair and the MFA Forum were very different. The MFA Forum targeted governments and corporations – although the term 'target' implies more confrontational rhetoric than is actually apparent in MFA Forum documents. It would be more accurate to say that governments and corporations are the intended recipients of the Forum's recommendations. By framing their recommendations in a particular way, and including government and business representatives as participants in the Forum, the organisers' fundamental strategy was apparently to move away from viewing multinational corporations as the targets and instead use more subtle forms of persuasion. The Play Fair campaign targeted the seven selected manufacturers and the sportswear industry as a whole.

Another aspect of information politics is the way in which the issues are 'framed', or presented to the public, and the meanings and sentiments that are attached to the issues. Play Fair was particularly successful on this front because of its association with the Olympics. The MFA Forum, on the other hand, was not necessarily directed at the general public and did not include a big public-awareness campaign. This is not necessarily a weakness of the Forum, since Forum participants were not trying to mobilise the public to undertake or support a singular, clear course of action.

The main way in which the MFA Forum employed information politics and framed the issues was to emphasise co-operative engagement among NGOs, trade unions, government agencies, and businesses in an effort to develop 'win–win' solutions whereby businesses can remain profitable without sacrificing workers' rights and access to decent livelihoods. In terms of information politics, the MFA Forum used its engagement with corporations to bolster its legitimacy with the private sector. Persuading corporations to negotiate seems to be an important strategy of the MFA Forum. Providing credible information encouraged private-sector involvement in the Forum. The danger is that either the corporations involved will benefit from the positive public relations generated from their participation, without actually initiating any substantial change, or that the NGOs involved will be overpowered by the participating businesses and lose their ability to advocate successfully on behalf of affected workers and communities.

Symbolic politics

Symbolic politics is the 'ability to call upon symbols, actions, or stories that make sense of a situation for an audience that is frequently far away' (Keck and Sikkink 1998:16). Both campaigns focused on specific events or situations, Play Fair on the 2004 Olympics, and the MFA Forum on the phasing-out of the Multifibre Arrangement. Play Fair, in particular, used symbolic politics effectively by linking exploitation in the sportswear industry with the Olympic Games. Many people follow the Olympics on TV and think of the event as a celebration of goodwill and global co-operation. By highlighting the exploitation of workers who make clothing for the Olympics, the Play Fair organisers demonstrated the hypocrisy of sportswear companies' claims to global goodwill.

The MFA Forum, on the other hand, could not take advantage of similar symbolic and emotional associations. The realm of trade and trade agreements, while extraordinarily powerful in influencing the livelihoods of millions of people, is not particularly exciting and offers few accessible topics to engage the general public in the North. For that reason, trade issues such as the MFA do not often resonate with the general public. Other campaigns, however, such as those calling for debt relief, have been more successful in 'framing' the issues and communicating with the public; a recent example is the Live 8 concerts, held around the world to coincide with the G8 Summit in Scotland in July 2005. Along with vibrant social movements, these seemingly technical issues can be 'reframed' as front-page news.

Leverage politics

Keck and Sikkink (*op.cit.*: 16) describe leverage politics as the 'ability to call upon powerful actors to affect a situation where weaker members of a network are unlikely to have influence'. The MFA Forum's ability to include The Gap, Nike, and Marks & Spencer is evidence of the successes of previous campaigns targeted at each of these corporations. It is likely that previous pressure and the need to improve their public images led these companies to the MFA Forum table. This may illustrate the long-term nature of campaigns, where even small successes are the result of many actions by many different actors over a long period of time.

According to Keck and Sikkink, networks can seek leverage over more powerful institutions in two forms: material and moral. Material leverage 'usually links the issue to money and goods' (*op. cit.*: 23). The Play Fair campaign effectively used material leverage by focusing on the corporations' vulnerabilities, namely their public image and branding. Sponsorships for the 2004 Olympics were valued at $648 million (Oxfam 2004: 33). Corporations are vulnerable to strategies that seek to tarnish their image, because they rely heavily on the positive image and subsequent earnings that sponsorships are designed to achieve. Play Fair organisers chose the seven companies because of their level of brand recognition, rather than focusing on suppliers that may be unfamiliar to consumers. The only problem with this strategy is that sometimes the most familiar brands are targeted, in preference to a focus on the most flagrant abusers who may not have the same brand recognition among Northern consumers. Consumers could incorrectly assume that export-oriented producers are guilty of more flagrant abuses than their domestic counterparts, which is not necessarily the case (Hutchison 2004). However, using leverage politics in this case depends on being able to make close links between production and consumption. This is much harder to do with non-exporting manufacturers (Merk 2005d).

Moral leverage 'involves what some commentators have called the "mobilization of shame," where the behaviour of target actors is held up to the light of international scrutiny' (Keck and Sikkink 1998: 23). Shame also has material consequences for corporations. By linking exploitation of workers with the Olympics, the Play Fair campaign mobilised shame and cast a shadow on the goodwill (and big business) associated with sponsorships. The MFA Forum did not have the same kind of access to either material or moral leverage in order to pressure buyers, suppliers, or governments to act decisively. This is partly because the issues raised by the Multifibre Arrangement are still being framed, but also because of the complexity of the issues and differences of opinions on trade liberalisation in general, and on the MFA in particular, even among participants of the Forum.

Accountability politics

The last type of tactics described by Keck and Sikkink (1998: 16) is accountability politics, or 'the effort to hold powerful actors to their previously stated policies or principles'. Some of the organisers of Play Fair, such as the Clean Clothes Campaign and Oxfam, have had success with accountability politics in other campaigns. For example, once corporations join the Fair Labor Association (almost always as a concession following effective pressuring and lobbying from NGOs and consumers), they are held to higher standards, including monitoring for compliance. The problem, of course, is that this deters corporations from agreeing to make any changes, because they know that they will be held to higher standards once they enter into dialogue with activists. The Play Fair campaign was successful in getting Asics to join the Fair Labor Association; however, it is not yet clear whether others such as Umbro will do so (Merk 2005d). Campaign organisers may be able to take advantage of the cyclical nature of the Olympics and other sporting events such as the World Cup, exercising accountability politics with these same corporations, reporting on progress made (if any) by the targeted companies (Merk 2005c).

The MFA Forum had some opportunities to use accountability politics, particularly by highlighting the hypocrisy of Northern governments that impose significant trade barriers on developing countries while at the same time heavily subsidising domestic industries. However, the Forum did not use this strategy, preferring to adopt a more conciliatory tone, rather than drawing attention to the gaps between free-trade rhetoric and practice.

Gender politics

Even though assessing each campaign according to the politics of information, symbolism, leverage, and accountability can help us to learn about the tactics employed by the organisers, this does not tell the whole story. What is missing is an analysis of the *gender politics* of each campaign, in order to assess the potential for gender and development practitioners and activists to make effective use of transnational advocacy networks.

Both the MFA Forum and Play Fair addressed issues that affect poor women, particularly women working in the global garment industry. While neither campaign claimed to represent or speak for poor women, women workers were seen as the 'beneficiaries' of their efforts, although this was not always made explicit. A problematic aspect of both campaigns, and one that continues to plague social movements and transnational advocacy networks, many of which are based in the North, is the lack of representation of the so-called beneficiaries in decision-making processes. This is not to say that poor women were not consulted; they were in both cases. However, in both Play Fair and the MFA Forum, women garment workers did not play significant decision-making roles.

Although the purpose of the Play Fair campaign was to improve the working conditions for workers in the sportswear industry, the majority of whom are women, the Play Fair documents do not include extensive analysis of the systematic exploitation of garment workers as women, beyond a short section in the Play Fair report about hiring women, migrants, and temporary workers. The report does quote female workers' testimony about the abuses that they face in the factories, including sexual harassment, inadequate sick and maternity leave, and the occurrence of miscarriages due to over-work, but the predominant themes are 'gender-neutral', focusing on workers' exploitation in terms of forced overtime and their inability to join unions.

Much of the language associated with the Play Fair campaign was that of the larger anti-sweatshop movement, focusing strictly on labour conditions and freedom of association, rather than the wider gender-related implications for women working in the industry. Gender-neutral language may have helped to illustrate worker solidarities across countries, but the problem is that these issues are not gender-neutral. Jeroen Merk (2005d) argues that freedom of assembly is not gender-neutral, because it 'is necessary to give women workers a voice in many issues that directly affect them on the workfloor', and 'through freedom of assembly women workers potentially can start to negotiate working conditions from a gendered perspective with management'.

Neither campaign has portrayed women workers as voiceless victims, but nor did they thoroughly empower women workers to be vocal in decision-making roles. According to Kidder (2002) many women's organisations that engage in advocacy on labour issues tend to address the non-financial issues that affect women, such as additional pressures from family and society, in addition to the financial ones; whereas more traditional union-led efforts tend to focus exclusively on financial matters within the workplace. Some of this may have been strategic on the part of Play Fair and MFA Forum organisers. After all, it is easier to pressure companies to obey overtime legislation than it is to change society's perceptions about the value of women's paid and unpaid labour. Yet both are necessary.

Several of the MFA Forum documents, especially *Mapping the End of the MFA*, do include analysis of the gendered impacts of the phasing out of the quota system. The report acknowledges that the majority of garment workers in most countries are women. According to the MFA Forum, many of these women, who are often young, unmarried migrants to urban areas from rural villages, will have difficulty finding alternative sources of employment if factories close. The report also mentions the difficulties that women workers face in terms of the cultural significance attached to garment work. As an example, the report claims that in Sri Lanka some marriage advertisements include the statement 'Factory girls need not reply'. The *Mapping* document includes findings from Women Working Worldwide, Oxfam, and the Maquila Solidarity Network, all of which are engaged with women working in the garment industry and may be able to insert further gender analysis into future documents and analysis produced by the MFA Forum.

Just as trade agreements have had different and unequal effects on men and women due to their lack of gender sensitivity or analysis, the 'solutions' will most likely have gendered implications too. Ignoring the gendered dynamics of trade and labour is problematic for several reasons. First, it replicates problems apparent in initial trade agreements and corporate policies that either ignored gender altogether or made unthinking and prejudiced assumptions about women. Second, it means that these campaigns are missing an opportunity to make connections and build solidarity with other activists in global women's movements. The goal is not to have 'gender' as an added category in a footnote of a report, but instead to incorporate the needs, desires, and demands of workers – even if they are gender-specific (i.e. maternity leave, child care, adequate wages as primary earners) – and embed them in the campaigns and create links with those involved in gender and development advocacy around the world.

Conclusion

While neither campaign achieved dramatic, instantaneous, industry-wide change, both were successful in giving prominence to issues that had previously been ignored. By linking fair labour practices with the Olympics, the Play Fair campaign was able to highlight exploitative labour practices at a time when the sportswear industry was counting on generating a positive image and strong brand recognition. The MFA Forum built a collaborative alliance of NGOs, unions, and businesses to begin to discuss the consequences of the MFA phase-out. The full effects of both campaigns have not yet been realised. Long-term success can be gauged only with the culmination of many campaigns, activities, and actions over time.

In addition to highlighting the potential for transnational advocacy networks engaged in gender and economic justice, the two cases illustrate important challenges that transnational advocacy networks face in order to fully achieve cross-border, trans-formative change. The MFA tried to address one such challenge – the difficulty of access to intergovernment bodies and multinational corporations – through its collaborative framework. Internal challenges within networks can arise from inequities among actors within networks, conflicts over resources, organisational or personal conflicts, disagreements about identities or priorities, and disagreements about goals and strategies, as well as the practical difficulties of meeting, collaborating, and communicating across the globe (Bandy and Smith 2005: 237).

The lessons learned from Play Fair and the MFA Forum can help gender and development practitioners and activists to employ informational, symbolic, leverage, accountability, and gender politics strat-egically in transnational advocacy networks

to challenge corporate-driven globalisation. Even though the two campaigns employed very different tactics and strategies, they are both part of vibrant transnational advocacy networks which aim to improve conditions for workers in the garment industry around the globe. This is particularly important in the post-MFA era, because competition among the least-developed countries to retain a segment of the garment industry could mean harsher working conditions and lower wages for millions of women working on the global assembly line.

Shae Garwood is a PhD candidate in the Discipline of Political Science and International Relations at the University of Western Australia. She holds the degree of Master of Science in Gender and Development Studies from the London School of Economics and Political Science. She can be contacted at garwos01@student.uwa.edu.au or Discipline of Political Science, School of Social and Cultural Studies, University of Western Australia, 35 Stirling Highway, Crawley, WA 6009, Australia.

Notes

The author thanks Barb Gottlieb, of the Women's Edge Coalition, and Alexandra Spieldoch, of International Gender and Trade Network, for providing valuable background information used in this article.

1 Numerous organisations and campaigns are engaged in advocacy for gender and economic justice, such as the International Gender and Trade Network, Oxfam's Make Trade Fair Campaign, Women's Edge, the Clean Clothes Campaign, Transnational Information Exchange, Women Working Worldwide, and the Maquila Solidarity Network. They employ a variety of strategies to achieve gender and economic justice in the garment industry, including sharing information and technical assistance,

raising awareness among the public and policy makers, directly lobbying decision makers, strengthening and supporting unions, and encouraging shareholder activism.

2 Participants in the Forum include AccountAbility, Business for Social Responsibility, Co-operative Group, Ethical Trading Initiative, Fair Labor Association, Fundemas, Gap Inc., George/ASDA, Interfaith Centre on Corporate Responsibility, International Textiles, Garment & Leather Workers' Federation, Littlewoods, Marks & Spencer, Maquila Solidarity Network, Nike, Oxfam International, Social Accountability International, UNDP Asia Trade Initiative, UN Global Compact, and the World Bank Group. The author was unable to interview Forum participants for this article.

3 The organisers of the campaign – the Clean Clothes Campaign, Oxfam, and Global Unions – are each conglomerations of various other individuals and organisations. The Clean Clothes Campaign (CCC) 'is an international coalition of consumer organizations, trade unions, researchers, human rights groups, solidarity activists, migrant, homeworker, and women workers' organizations, Fair Trade Shops and many other organizations, which aims to improve working conditions in the global garment industry'. Based in 11 European countries, CCC has approximately 250 member organisations and works closely with partner organisations in many garment-producing countries. Oxfam is a confederation of affiliated organisations working in more than 100 countries, aiming to find 'lasting solutions to poverty and injustice'. Eleven Oxfam affiliates participated in the Play Fair campaign. Global Unions includes 'the major institutions of the international trade union movement', consisting of the International Confederation of Free Trade Unions, ten Global Union Federations, and the Trade Union Advisory Committee to the OECD (Oxfam 2004).

References

Accountability (2005) 'Mapping the End of the MFA', www.mfa-forum.net/ (last checked 23 September 2005).

Bandy, J. and J. Smith (2005) *Coalitions Across Borders*, New York: Rowman & Littlefield.

Brooke, J. (2005) 'Trade quotas? Ah, the good old days', *The New York Times*, 9 April 2005.

Business for Social Responsibility (2004) 'The Multi-Fiber Arrangement: Strategic Sourcing Impact, The Private Sector Perspective, Business for Social Responsibility'.

Chan, A. (2003) 'A 'race to the bottom': globalisation and China's labour standards', *China Perspectives* 46 (March/April).

Connor, T. (2004) 'Time to scale up cooperation? Trade unions, NGOs, and the international anti-sweatshop movement', *Development in Practice* 14 (1&2): 61-70.

Ethical Trading Initiative (2005) 'Ethical Trading Initiative Welcomes Output of Dhaka Conference', ETI Press Release, www.ethicaltrade.org/z/lib/2005/06/mfa-press-dhaka2/index.shtml (last checked 20 July 2005).

Elson, D. and R. Pearson (1981) 'Nimble fingers make cheap workers: an analysis of women's employment in third world export manufacturing', *Feminist Review* (Spring): 87-107.

Foo, L. and N. Bas (2003) 'Free Trade's Looming Threat to the World's Garment Workers', Oakland: Sweatshop Watch Working Paper.

Goodman, P. (2005) 'China resists U.S. pressure on textiles, currency', *The Washington Post*, 28 May 2005.

Hutchison, J. (2004) 'Export Opportunities: Women Workers Organising in the Philippine Garment Industry', PhD Thesis: Murdoch University, www.lib.murdoch.edu.au/adt/browse/view/adt-MU20050201.155254 (last checked 24 July 2005).

International Labour Organization (2000) 'Labour Practices in the Footwear, Leather, Textiles and Clothing Industry,' Geneva: International Labour Organization.

Iritani, E. and M. Dickerson (2005) 'Workers' rights at risk', *Los Angeles Times,* 17 January 2005.

Iritani, E., M. Dickerson, and T. Marshall (2005) 'When fear follows fabric along the assembly line', *Los Angeles Times*, 17 January 2005.

Kearney, N. (2005) 'Avoiding Meltdown in the Post-MFA World', International Textile and Garment and Leather Workers' Federation press release, 1 July 2005, www.itglwf.org/displaydocument.asp?DocType=Press&Language=&Index=1271 (last checked 16 July 2005).

Keck, M. and K. Sikkink (1998) *Activists Beyond Borders*, Ithaca: Cornell University Press.

Kidder, T. (2002) 'Networks in transnational labor organizing', in S. Khagram et al. (eds.) *Restructuring World Politics*, Minneapolis: University of Minnesota.

Marshall, T., E. Iritani, and M. Dickerson (2005) 'Clothes will cost less, but some nations pay', *Los Angeles Times*, 16 January 2005.

Merk, J. (2005a) 'The Play Fair at the Olympics Campaign: An evaluation of the company responses', Clean Clothes Campaign, ICFTU, Oxfam.

Merk, J. (2005b) personal communication (via email), 13 June 2005.

Merk, J. (2005c) interview (via phone), 8 July 2005.

Merk, J. (2005d) personal communication (via email), 25 August 2005.

MFA Forum (2005a) www.mfa-forum.org (last checked 30 June 2005).

MFA Forum (2005b) 'A Collaborative Framework for Guiding Post-MFA Actions'.

Miller, D. (2005) 'A Play Fair Alliance Evaluation of the WFSGI Response to the Play Fair at the Olympics Campaign'.

Murthy, L. (2004) 'Play Fair at the Olympics', Infochange News and Features, http://infochangeindia.org/features209.jsp (lst checked 3 July 2005).

Oxfam (2004) *Play Fair at the Olympics: Respect workers' rights in the sportswear industry*, Oxford: Oxfam GB, Clean Clothes Campaign, ICFTU.

Gender networking and advocacy work in Uganda:
controlling the agenda and strategies of resistance

Mary Ssonko Nabacwa

Relations between donors and national NGOs undertaking gender advocacy are very complex. The same is true of relations between the advocacy networks, their member NGOs, and women at the grassroots. This study draws on research carried out by the author for her doctorate. The research considers advocacy to promote gender equality, and shows how this activity both affects, and is shaped by, the power relationships among the various actors involved. It examines the relationships between various actors in Uganda who have an interest in advocacy on gender issues: donors, international and local NGOs, and members of grassroots communities. Both donors and national NGOs accept that there is a need for advocacy, to raise the profile of key gender issues and to try to influence policy and practice. However, they have different motives for doing this work, and their agendas may diverge from each other at times. Ultimately this affects the quality of the work that they do to represent the interests of Ugandan women.

Working in coalitions, partnerships, and alliances to pursue advocacy objectives is currently fashionable. Networks set up to achieve international and national advocacy objectives involve both local and international organisations. Because of the role of international NGOs as donors, these relationships involve unequal power relations, and sometimes conditions can be imposed by the powerful, who promote certain agendas. However, in addition to collaborating and complying with the more powerful players, the less powerful can resist. The choices that both players make affect the advocacy work undertaken.

This article[1] examines the Ugandan experience of networking designed to promote gender equality through advocacy. The formation of networks at the instigation of international bodies has had several major effects on local NGO relationships in Uganda. An increased number of local NGOs focusing on gender and women's issues are now engaged in advocacy work – actively or passively – via their membership of newly formed networks. In Uganda, several gender-equality networks have been funded and promoted by one or more international NGO. The article focuses on one such network: the Uganda Women's Network (UWONET). It traces the relations of competition and co-operation which exist between this body and its member organisations, and the network's relations of patronage with its donors. Each of these actors is motivated by very different interests.

Donors can be divided into two broad categories in the Ugandan context. The first category is small donors (international NGOs); the second is the big bilateral and multilateral donors, who are usually called 'official' donors (Edwards 2002). I use the analysis of Edwards as an aid to understanding the NGO–donor relation-ships within these networks. He argues that, in relation to advocacy work, 'the real strength of Northern NGOs [international NGOs, in the terms of my study] lies in their simultaneous access to grassroots experience in the South and to decision makers in the North' (*ibid.*: 98). International NGOs depend on local NGOs for illustrations and evidence of the points that they wish to make in advocacy at the international level. It is critically important to them to obtain the right information, in a cost-effective way, and package it appropriately to make it suitable for advocacy purposes. International NGOs need to develop institutional structures that will enable all this to happen in a timely manner. This involves the creation of national-level structures such as networks and coalitions, which are perceived to be the best means of furthering the advocacy agenda.

Features of donor-nurtured advocacy networks

'Familial' relations

A feature of relationships between small donors and national NGOs who work together in alliances is pseudo-familial relations. International NGOs' relations with local NGOs tend to have a lasting influence on the activities and operation of the networks and their member organisations, and many participate as 'senior partners' in the activities of these networks. This is especially true in advocacy networks which the international NGOs have helped to create in the first place. These relationships are by and large cordial, and relatively unconfrontational.

A key aspect of familial relations is nurturing and producing. In advocacy networks this is often expressed in terms of the influence wielded by international NGOs over the areas of operation of networks and alliances. They do this by organising the writing and application of country strategy papers, which use the conceptual and analytical frameworks employed by the international NGOs. Local NGOs are expected to adopt, and perhaps contribute to, these guiding discourses. International NGOs take a senior role in network meetings and workshops, and undertake training work to 'build the capacity' of local organisations. In certain cases in Uganda, the international NGOs directly influence the areas of operation of the networks. International NGOs may also carry out research in 'partnership' with local agencies.

UWONET is an example of a donor-nurtured network in Uganda. UWONET acts as a membership-based advocacy organisation for women's organisations. Other interested organisations may be enrolled as associates. UWONET is a product of the Ugandan preparations for the Fourth United Nations Conference on Women, held in Beijing in 1995. Following the Third UN Conference on Women, which was held in Nairobi in 1990, some donors who were working closely with women's organisations in Uganda looked around for a vibrant women's organisation in Uganda which could move beyond traditional welfare programming. Donors in Uganda felt the need for an umbrella organisation, or network, which would be willing to venture into work that involved challenges to structural gender inequality, and in the process would build the capacity of its member organisations (interview, M., June 2003).

Because such an organisation had not yet come into being, donors reasoned that they needed to set about nurturing one. In their turn, local NGOs focusing on women's issues recognised the need to work together. UWONET's members agreed to form a 'loose network with a focal point to which the member organisations would convene to review progress on priority issues and the members were to play the lead role' (UWONET 1996). One of the founders of the network, who used to work in a donor agency, commented in an interview with the present author that *'we had an idea of a small advocacy unit, a secretariat not supposed to become an NGO'* (interview, M., June 2003). The network was seen as a strategic rallying point for women's organisations for addressing gender inequalities, focusing on women's strategic rather than practical needs.

UWONET's members did not want to bring an independent umbrella organisation into being, fearing that it would compete with them for resources (UWONET 1996). Competition for resources among NGOs is caused by the market/buyer relations between NGOs and donors, described in the next section.

Buyer/seller relations

Relationships between donors and local NGOs can be characterised in terms of those between buyer and seller.[2] The sellers are the local NGOs, who constantly adjust their 'brand' – that is, their programmes and their guiding discourses – to fit the demands of the buyers (the donors). This is a relationship of domination, in which local NGOs fear losing the donors. Domination is expressed through the donors' requirement that local NGOs should conform to financial-accountability mechanisms and other frameworks such as proposal formats and monitoring and evaluation mechanisms. Donors can also determine the broad themes on which NGOs may work, and determine the kinds of result that NGOs work towards, and the scheduling of their work. This results in the NGOs having increasingly limited room for manoeuvre.

Edwards (2002) suggests that relationships in such situations are characterised by mistrust and confrontation. Local NGOs do not really trust their donors, and they may use both direct and indirect means to confront them. Indirect means are favoured, because they are less risky. They use spaces that are perceived to be safe ground on which to confront donors: for example, conferences, workshops, or research. During my research they expressed sentiments such

as: *'Development partners? They are donors, it is not a relationship. He who pays the piper calls the tune. They pay the piper, they call the tune. It is an unhealthy relationship'* (interview, O., June 2003).

In the next section I consider relationships between local NGOs in the networks.

Relations between local NGOs in advocacy networks

NGOs in Uganda seem well aware of the complexity of their relationships with donors, and have devised their own coping mechanisms to maximise their interests. My research findings showed that while donors may be dominant in the NGO/donor relationships in advocacy networks, NGOs use strategies to limit donor power in the networks, and maximise their own access to donor resources. In this section I discuss some of the strategies used.

These strategies are characterised by relations of competition and resistance among the NGOs, caused by a need for resources (which are limited), plus the need to assert status and identity. Both these factors enhance the likelihood of receiving funds from donors. Competition is greater among NGOs with similar interests and characteristics. Such competition manifests itself in both overt and hidden ways. Much competition is hidden from view and can be inferred only by reading the organisational documents and interviewing a cross-section of staff and members of the selected NGOs.

In the case of UWONET, there was hidden competition between the network as an entity in its own right and its member organisations (MOs). There was also competition between member organisations. Yet the relationships were also characterised by co-operation. These dynamics are discussed below.

Relations of competition

The competition between UWONET and the members has gone on for a very long time. It was envisaged at the early stages of the network that 'the operations of the network do not and should not weaken the autonomy of its members' (UWONET 1996). However, the process required for registration made the network an independent legal entity in its own right. The hiring of staff by the network enhanced its independence from its members. This marked the beginning of stiffened and persistent competition between UWONET and its members. As already noted, the members wanted a network that depended on them. But it was evident that, due to its registration as an NGO and its independent receipt of resources from its donors, the network had become a separate entity that indeed had the potential to compete with its member organisations for resources, identity, and status.

My research findings showed that the members have a 'love–hate' relationship with their network, depending on what they want, or what it wants from them. At times the network and MOs have agreed to collaborate, as a better alternative to competition. At other times, hostility, passive resistance, lack of involvement, and poor communications have dominated. The relations between the network and its members have played a critical role in shaping the gender-advocacy agenda of NGOs in Uganda.

Members of the network use various mechanisms in resistance. The first is to undermine the network in the eyes of donors. Fears and suspicion that the network will overshadow them or hijack their work are prevalent. The cause of competition and resistance is mainly the need for recognition. Member organisations fear that networks may put their name or logo on the members' work and claim the credit for it. The networks, as well as the members, need recognition of their input to the advocacy campaigns. With limited monitoring mechanisms, the closest proximity to measuring the impact of one's role in advocacy is the extent to which one is perceived to be advocating.

One way to resist the tendency for the network to become more prominent in its own right than its member organisations is to undermine the network, through provision of limited information and non-attendance at meetings of member organisations. Information is critical for effective advocacy planning. Limited information has put the network in precarious situations where it adopts a particular advocacy issue at the suggestion of the members, but is then forced to cease active advocacy because it has been provided with insufficient information to support the initiative. Another method of resistance is to duplicate activities: member organisations have organised their own advocacy activities, similar to those of the network.

In the context of these difficult relationships, to compensate for the members' lack of support and active involvement, UWONET's secretariat habitually makes decisions in its advocacy work without input from the members. UWONET's secretariat is aware that the key factor in the work of the network is the availability of donor funds. Since the network is important for donors' advocacy agendas, the input of the constituent members is desirable, but not essential. Assured funding means that whether the members support or do not support an idea, it will be implemented. Thus, while the members may resist the network by not attending meetings, or sending junior staff who are not decision makers, this is not necessarily an impediment to the continuity of the activity. It may affect the strategies used, but not the actual continuity of the activity itself.

However, while this strategy solves short-term problems, it creates further dissatisfactions among members, and provokes a quiet withdrawal of members who feel that they have no control over their network. UWONET has tried to improve its relations with its constituents by sharing its strategy and annual report with the member organisations, in which texts it acknowledges the member organisations' activities, to avoid claims that it is stealing their work.

Relations of co-operation

One person described the relationship between UWONET and its members as 'a marriage' in which there is some degree of allegiance. Even while the member organisations are often aware of problems and unhappy with the way the network uses its identity to build its own status and access resources, they continue to belong to it. The members believe in the issues that the network is working on. In an informal group discussion, my interviewees said that the problem is not the issues, but the mechanisms and strategies employed to handle the issues. They also pointed out that the members benefit from the network through profile raising and capacity development: for example, they learn advocacy skills, get ideas for strategies, and so on.

Member organisations clearly recognise the power of the network, in comparison with their own power as individual organisations. There was also recognition of the importance of the web of relations among the various actors, which are mainly nurtured and maintained by the networks. It enables organisations to deal with politically sensitive gender-related issues as a collective; members can take advantage of numerical superiority to challenge government and other centres of power. Providing a platform to share common concerns and speak with one voice on women's issues is important if the members are to become established players in the public debate.

There was also a feeling that members benefit from networks more generally – beyond advocacy – through the opportunity to publicise their work, and to learn. Networking provided opportunities to pool resources, although one research subject noted that, due to competing relations, the network has not taken full advantage of the human capacity that is available within its membership organisations. Another local

NGO worker said that networking provides a 'bigger voice', while another called it 'a collective voice'. A collective voice achieves greater results, and some members derive emotional and professional satisfaction from being members of the network.

There was also acknowledgement that networks provide opportunities to link with civil-society organisations more widely. This means that gender issues come to the attention of others. Community organisations, donor agencies, universities, and NGOs have all benefited from their interaction with the networks, and some have incorporated gender concerns and findings into the policies of these institutions. Thus, in spite of the unsatisfactory relations that have developed, the members' recognition of the importance of social capital nurtured by the networks and the alliance has persuaded most of them to maintain relations with the network.

While networking is valued by the various member organisations, members are also pragmatic: UWONET is very popular among donor organisations, and it is these donors that provide the life-blood of the member organisations. Hence, member organisations prefer co-operation to competition, because the latter may be costly to the identity and status of the individual member organisations, in terms of the respect, status, and recognition that they command with donors. Member organisations would not like to be identified by UWONET and their fellow members as unsupportive of the network.

Strategies for increasing co-operation and reducing competition

Some mechanisms for reducing competition and increasing collaboration within the network are noted here.

Building close relationships with local staff in donor agencies

Local staff in donor agencies are often in a strong position to influence and shape the agendas of donors, and their relationships with local NGOs. It is evident that the local staff in the donor agencies have a comparative advantage in relation to their counterparts because of their local knowledge. Local NGOs take advantage of relationships with such people, who can function as interlocutors, mediators, or even interpreters. They can also assist staff of local NGOs by advising them on ways of relating to donor agencies, or on adapting their agendas in line with the issues that are most likely to attract donor funding.

Building close relationships between staff in organisations within the network

Strong relationships between individuals can also strengthen networks. One research subject said that the relationship between the individuals within the various organisations in UWONET had been critical in ensuring organisational support for the network's activities. In addition it was important for staff of UWONET to develop strong relationships with individuals, because this helped the secretariat to understand the various member organisations and how to relate to them. Informal individual relations are important in agenda setting and management. One interviewee from UWONET commented: *'When you look at the organisations that we really worked with, I made them to be personal friends, that you know them beyond the organisations'* (interview, R., July 2003).

However, individual relationships have their own shortcomings. One research subject noted that when the mutual trust was based on a relationship between individuals, this did not filter through to wider relationships between their organisations. This factor created discontinuity when those individuals left their organisations. In addition to problems of discontinuity, one research subject told me that the process of developing relations between individual 'buddies' resulted in the formation of cliques, which made some other individuals who represented their organisations in

UWONET feel isolated and unimportant. The cliques were mainly based on similarities in age or ethnic origin, or on shared histories: for example, they were formed by people who had all attended the same school. The cliques also made agenda formulation less transparent and democratic, so that the views of only a few individuals tended to prevail.

Organisation of joint initiatives

In order to overcome the mistrust between the members and the network, while meeting the needs of the donors, a network secretariat and any of the member organisations may agree to organise collaborative advocacy activities. UWONET's members were not willing to share their information with the network freely, and accused it of stealing their information. On the other hand, the UWONET secretariat accused its members of using the information from the network meetings to make individual proposals intended to impress donors and obtain funding. To address this problem, UWONET had tried organising its advocacy initiatives in collaboration with a member organisation, so that they could both report on the same activity. This helped them both to manage concerns about accountability to donors, while ensuring the donors' recognition of the contribution of particular players.

This last point is particularly important, since undertaking joint programmes can be problematic. Some donor agencies require member organisations to show tangible results. This may lead to conflict among member organisations in competition for results and recognition, and the fear that their identity might be swallowed by the network (UWONET 1999). The same concern was noted by one research subject, who said that donors' accountability mechanisms made it difficult to ensure that member organisations who might have a comparative advantage in undertaking a particular activity were actually free to do so, since donors expected accountability from the organisation that originally received the funding (interview, R, June 2003).

The creation of issue-based sub-networks

The need in Uganda for advocacy on particular issues has led to the creation of sub-networks or coalitions, which amount to a restructuring of UWONET. Such groupings include the Domestic Relations Bill (DRB) Coalition, the Coalition of Politics and Women (COPAW), and the Coalition Against Violence Against Women (CIVAW coalition). Although dominated by women's organisations, membership in all these different kinds of network is open to gender-focused NGOs (both international and local), government institutions, and individuals. UWONET provides leadership in all these coalitions and forums.

Conclusions

Networks set up to pursue a shared interest in challenging structural gender inequality offer an opportunity to member organisations to increase the impact of their work. However, at times the relations between the networks and some of their members become relations of political convenience for both parties. This article has attempted to uncover some of the unequal power dynamics that exist in one Ugandan network, UWONET. Local NGOs are in constant fear of losing funds from donors, either because the donors' priorities change, or because of their own poor accountability in terms of activities and funds. Relations of patronage result in strained relations among the various actors.

The article has argued that competition among the NGOs involved in UWONET manifested itself in both overt and hidden ways. Much competition was hidden, and could be uncovered only by reading and comparing organisational documents, and

interviewing a cross-section of staff and members of the selected NGOs. The fear of overt dissent from donor agendas was also obvious to me when I presented my research findings to a cross-section of NGO staff in Uganda. While they were interested in my findings, they were also mindful of the implications for donor funding. The NGOs did not want to expose what was going on in their organisations and networks, just in case the donors decided to stop funding them.

In conclusion, local NGOs may run risks of being co-opted by big donors into support for agendas which they do not share. Becoming a member of a donor-supported network can have a dramatic effect on the programmes of the membership organisation. Commitment to advocacy and the presence of powerful networks and coalitions at the national level does not necessarily translate into processes of change at the grassroots level. In Uganda, local NGOs feel obliged to sustain and support UWONET, since it is the donors' baby – even if they do not like the baby's behaviour. Probably if their relations with the donor were less dependent, they would have nurtured this baby differently. Understanding the power relationships (formal and informal, hidden and overt) between organisations is critical to our understanding of advocacy on gender-related concerns in developing-country contexts. Lack of resources, the need for recognition, status, and identity, and the current politics of aid are key determinants of the ways in which these relationships are shaped and manifest themselves. The way in which the NGOs involved – and individuals within them – manage these relationships has major implications for the extent to which the agendas of gender-equality advocacy reflect the interests of women at the grassroots.

Mary Ssonko Nabacwa is a PhD student at the Centre for Development Studies, University of Wales Swansea, c/o Centre for Development Studies, University of Wales, Swansea, SA2 8PP, 151840@swansea.ac.uk

Notes

1 This article is based on work for the author's on-going PhD study at the University of Wales, Swansea. For permission to publish it here we acknowledge the NGO Practice Research Team, which included it in a report on Uganda for ESCOR, DFID, by Tina Wallace and others (see www.ngopractice.org).

2 Buyer/seller relations are characteristic of relations between local NGOs and major, bilateral, or multilateral donors. The research subjects in my study expressed concern that donors are funding NGOs which act as safety-nets for people who are suffering the impact of the macro-economic policies that the major donors have themselves supported in Uganda. *'Many official donors only want to ensure that the policies do not adversely affect the poor, but they want to continue with their economic and social policies; local NGOs then become agents of these agencies'* (interview, J., June 2003).

References

Edwards M. (2002) '"Does the doormat influence the boot?" Critical thoughts on UK NGOs and international advocacy', in D. Eade (ed.) *Development and Advocacy, Selected Essays from Development in Practice,* Oxford: Oxfam GB, 2002

UWONET (1996) 'Reflection Retreat', Mbarara

UWONET (1999) External Evaluation Report

The African Women's Protocol: a new dimension for women's rights in Africa

Rose Gawaya and Rosemary Semafumu Mukasa

This article discusses the development and agreement of the African Women's Protocol, adopted by African Heads of State in 2003. The authors consider the experience of Oxfam GB in supporting the development and ratification of the Protocol. They make particular reference to the southern African countries of Mozambique, South Africa, and Zambia.

The Protocol to the African Charter on Human and People's Rights on the Rights of Women in Africa (known as 'The African Women's Protocol') was adopted by African Heads of State in July 2003, at the Maputo Summit of the African Union, held in Mozambique. The Protocol is significant in three ways. It reinforces the status of women's rights that have been established and elaborated in other international and regional instruments. But it is also the first instrument in international law explicitly to enshrine women's sexual and reproductive rights to medical abortion when pregnancy results from rape or incest, or when the continuation of pregnancy endangers the health of a mother. It is the first instrument in international law to call for the legal prohibition of female genital mutilation. And it is the first instrument of its kind developed by Africans, for Africans.

This article discusses the experience of Oxfam GB (hereafter referred to as 'Oxfam')

in supporting the development and ratification of the African Women's Protocol. Oxfam sees the Protocol as a tool for integrating gender-equality perspectives within its own programmes in the region, and as a means of influencing policy at national and local levels. Oxfam is part of a 19-member coalition of organisations in Africa, working to popularise the notion of the African Women's Protocol and lobby for its ratification and use by all African countries. The coalition has engaged in a number of activities, including launching a text-message campaign, attending African Union summits for lobbying purposes, and producing publications to raise awareness of the Protocol and the issues that it aims to address. Although it is not easy to assess the impact of these activities accurately, the coalition considers that its activities have contributed significantly to increasing the number of countries that have ratified the Protocol.

Oxfam's membership of the coalition forms part of the organisation's Pan African

Programme (PAPP), which is an advocacy initiative that aims to amplify African voices on issues affecting the continent. The programme focuses on three broad themes: governance, trade, and capacity building. Oxfam regards the PAPP as complementary to its work with grassroots communities. In its southern Africa programme, Oxfam works with partner organisations in six countries. The programme focuses, in particular, on supporting the livelihoods of women and men in poverty, and on helping them to find ways to reduce the impact of HIV/AIDS on their households and communities. Experience of working with women in poverty demonstrates clearly the need for laws and policies which are non-discriminatory and which support women to realise their full rights and entitlements as citizens. Oxfam believes that its PAPP activities complement the organisation's other advocacy activities, directed at inter-national and Northern targets. In this way, it seeks to create a truly global call for change.

Research on the African Women's Protocol and its significance for women's rights

The July 2004 Heads of State Summit Declaration on gender equality noted with concern the many obstacles faced by African women which prevent them exercising and enjoying their full human rights. The obstacles include conflict, poverty, and the impact of the HIV/AIDS pandemic. Women are subject to gender-based violence, including harmful traditional practices. Women continue to be numbered disproportionately among illiterate people in almost all African countries, a fact which reflects girls' limited access to education. Women also continue to be largely excluded from formal political participation, and they participate on an unequal basis in other decision-making processes in society.

The African Women's Protocol has 32 articles, covering social, cultural, economic, legal, and political concerns. It commits countries that sign and ratify it to adopt all measures necessary for women to be able to enjoy their human rights, including the provision of resources to make this possible. So far, 38 out of the 53 member states have signed the Protocol. Of these, eleven countries had ratified the Protocol at the time of writing.[1] The July 2004 Heads of State Summit Declaration urged States to sign and ratify the Protocol by the end of 2004, and to support the launching of public campaigns to ensure its entry into force by 2005. However, the Women's Protocol cannot come into force until 15 member states have ratified it. The need to ratify the Women's Protocol was reiterated at the second session of the Pan African Parliament in Midrand, South Africa, in September 2004).

Oxfam conducted research between November 2004 and May 2005 on the implications that the African Women's Protocol would have for women in the southern Africa region. The purpose of the policy research was to inform policy makers and implementers about the Protocol and its role in supporting gender equality and women's rights. The policy makers and implementers whom we were targeting included parliamentarians in the national and Pan African parliaments, officials of the African Union, and government officials. The research also aimed to raise public awareness of the Protocol's implications for women in Africa, and to strengthen the on-going campaigns run by other organisations in connection with the Women's Protocol.

Oxfam's research focused on Mozambique, South Africa, and Zambia. It included a comparative analysis of the Protocol and other international and regional laws and policies. It examined women's ability to assert their right to freedom from violence, and to sexual and reproductive rights, and women's role in governance.[2] Key findings are discussed below.

Comparing the Protocol with other laws and policies

The African Women's Protocol builds on prior legal agreements, aiming to promote and protect women's rights in a number of significant ways. It supports women confronting problems that were not addressed in either CEDAW (the 1979 Convention on All Forms of Discrimination Against Women), or the African Charter on Human and People's Rights. These problems include violence against women, HIV/AIDS, and denial of women's health and reproductive rights. The Protocol also widens the definition of crimes against humanity to include rape, sexual slavery, and other forms of sexual violence. It is clear that the Protocol is an advanced tool for protecting the rights of women in particularly vulnerable situations – for example, widows, older women, and pregnant and nursing mothers.

The African Women's Protocol differs from previous legal agreements in another sense: it is home-grown, developed by Africans for Africans. In some parts of Africa, women activists have considered CEDAW's effectiveness to be weakened by its perception as a legal instrument of Western women. On the other hand, the Protocol avoids the problems of the African Charter on Human and People's Rights, which in the opinion of many African women activists was excessively positive in its endorsement of African tradition, values, and customs. Because of this, it failed to acknowledge that some of these customs and traditions discriminate against – and harm – women.

The African Women's Protocol outlaws traditions such as female genital mutilation (FGM), widow inheritance, and child marriages. Furthermore, it does not stop at outlawing negative cultural practices, but goes on (in Article 17) to assert the right of African women to live in a 'positive cultural context' and their right to 'enhanced participation in the determination of cultural policies'. This article provides African women with a legal tool which can address one of their biggest challenges: the co-existence of customary and religious laws – which often discriminate against women – and civil law. Customary and religious laws often govern personal and family affairs, and often prevail over civil law and constitutional guarantees. This has been a major problem in implementing both CEDAW and the Beijing Platform for Action.

Another advantage of the African Women's Protocol is that it is legally binding. In this respect it differs from the Beijing Declaration and its associated Platform for Action, and from the Southern African Development Community (SADC) Gender Declaration and its Addendum on the Prevention and Eradication of Violence against Women and Children (1997). The Protocol reinforces CEDAW on a number of subjects, such as the trafficking of women, and the need to address inequalities in marriage with respect to decision making, inheritance of property, and parental rights. By calling for equal representation in decision making and political life, it further reinforces CEDAW, and improves on the 30 per cent target for women's representation that was set by the Beijing process and the SADC Declaration.

Women and NGOs can also make use of the rights enshrined in the Protocol to submit individual or group complaints to the African Commission on Human and People's Rights and to the African Court on Human and People's Rights (when the latter becomes operational – it is still unclear when this will be[3]). It therefore potentially provides for remedies to women whose rights have been violated. However, except in rare cases, individuals and other non-State actors do not have direct access to these mechanisms. Direct access is limited to cases where international instruments, once ratified, automatically become part of the country's national law.

Overall, the African Women's Protocol can strengthen the legal and policy framework of countries, and can help to promote action to protect the rights of women. It can help to bridge the gap between law and policy on the one hand, and practice and reality on the other. It can act as a shield against retrograde action which threatens women's rights, protecting the gains made by women in legal, political, economic, and social spheres.

Countries' responses to the Protocol

The research report considers in particular the implications of the Protocol for women in Mozambique, South Africa, and Zambia. It focuses on ways of enabling women to participate equally in governance, to resist and survive violence, and to monitor government spending through 'gender budgeting'; it also focuses on ways of involving men in work to support equal rights for women.

Political participation

Article 9 of the African Women's Protocol requires States that sign and ratify it to take specific positive action to promote the equal participation of women in governance and the political life of their countries. This affirmative action is intended to ensure that national legislation and other measures promote and support women's equal participation in elections, electoral processes, and the development and implementation of State policies and programmes.

Article 9 also requires States to increase the representation and participation of women at all levels of decision making, and ensure that this representation and participation are effective. The African Union has responded to the call for equal participation in decision making by appointing commissioners and elected women to high-level posts, such as the presidency of the Pan African Parliament. This sends out a positive signal to women.

The Protocol could be used to strengthen the regulatory framework for the participation of women in decision making, through legislation quotas and other affirmative-action measures. In South Africa, great strides have been made in the representation of women in decision making and political life, thanks to the 30 per cent quota currently applied as a voluntary measure by the African National Congress. However, such measures need to be formally incorporated into institutional policy and practice in order to ensure that they are sustained. Currently, they depend on the goodwill of the ruling party. Formal incorporation could also result in improvements in the practices of other political parties.

In Zambia, NGOs have proposed the introduction of quotas in their recommendations to the country's Constitutional Review Commission, in a bid to enhance the participation of women in politics. The Protocol could provide leverage for these efforts. In both South Africa and Zambia, the African Women's Protocol could also be used to spur much-needed progress in areas of governance such as local government, public service, the judiciary, the armed forces, and the private sector. The African Women's Protocol could also be used in advocacy work aiming to persuade institutions to put policies on equal participation into practice.

Violence against women

Article 4 of the African Women's Protocol commits States to enact and enforce laws to prohibit all forms of violence against women, whether it takes place in public or in private. States are obliged to adopt all appropriate measures to ensure the prevention and eradication of violence against women, and to punish perpetrators. The Protocol also commits governments to provide adequate budgets and other resources for the implementation and monitoring of these measures. This latter provision will be especially useful to women's rights activists in light of the fact that in all three countries resource constraints have been identified as a major challenge. In South Africa, the reference to budgetary resources has been widely praised. Article 4 also tackles the issue of the trafficking of women: a pervasive problem in the region, which none of the three countries has adequately addressed. The African Women's Protocol will support calls for more research, stronger legislation, appropriate policy, and more effective action in this area.

Article 5 prohibits and condemns all forms of harmful practices which negatively affect the human rights of women and are contrary to international standards. Women are still subject to harmful traditional practices in all three countries. To take the example of South Africa: the Constitution protects women from violence and harm and protects their rights to life, dignity, and health. However, no detailed policies exist on specific harmful practices such as female genital mutilation (FGM), virginity testing, 'dry sex' (the drying out of the vagina using chemical substances prior to sex, which increases vulnerability to injury during intercourse, and hence to sexually transmitted diseases), abduction or forced marriage, *ukungena* (taking over a widow by a male relative of the husband, without her consent), or burning and victimising women who have been branded 'witches'.

However, in dealing with harmful traditional practices, it will be important to define and build a consensus on what constitutes such practices. There are some practices in some areas on which there is no clear consensus, including *lobola* (bride-price), virginity testing, and some initiation rites. More research needs to be done on the impact of practices such as these, and a consensus must be built to define the circumstances under which some traditional practices become harmful, and how women can be protected.

Health and reproductive rights

Article 14 of the African Women's Protocol calls on States to ensure that women's right to health, including sexual and reproductive health, is respected and promoted. It provides women with the right to protection against sexually transmitted infections, including HIV/AIDS. It also authorises medical abortion in cases of sexual assault, rape, and incest, and where the continued pregnancy endangers the mental or physical health or life of the mother or foetus.

In South Africa, the Constitution provides women with unconditional rights to the termination of pregnancy. The Protocol therefore actually limits South African women's abortion rights. In contrast, in Zambia the Protocol is an advance on national legislation. Zambian women seeking medical abortion currently need a panel of three doctors to agree that the mother's health is threatened. If the mother's health is not threatened, Zambian law does not provide for termination, even in cases of rape, sexual assault, or incest.

Given the high prevalence of HIV/AIDS in the southern African region, the provisions of the Protocol on protection for women against HIV infection could help to improve the dire situation of women, since activists could adopt a rights-based argument, rather than the current welfare-focused arguments, in campaigning for more effective action. In all three countries, the emphasis on needs in rural areas in the Protocol's call for adequate, affordable, and accessible health services could help to bridge the wide disparity between services available to urban and rural women.

The focus on political participation, alongside other areas of concern, including reproductive and sexual health, confirms that the African Women's Protocol understands the link between the increased participation of women in decision making and socially responsible outcomes. Improved control over their fertility would free women to pursue more productive and fulfilling lives and would ensure healthier, more prosperous families. By addressing violence against women and harmful traditional practices that disempower them, the African Women's Protocol will help to improve living standards for both men and women.

Levels of awareness of the Protocol

Our research suggests that, on the whole, the level of public awareness about the African Women's Protocol is woefully low. Unfortunately, it was lowest among people working in the media, and community organisations. These are two groups who are crucial to its implementation. Most community organisations had never heard of the Protocol, and media coverage of the African Women's Protocol has been negligible. In South Africa, the ratification of the Protocol did not even make the news. The researchers did not find any reports about the ratification in newspapers or on TV or radio. There was no fanfare or public announcement. It was a missed opportunity for promoting public awareness about the Protocol.

In our view, the level of awareness was highest among individuals (government officials, members of parliament, and NGO workers) who have actually been involved in the promotion, adoption, and ratification of the Protocol. South Africans were more aware than Zambians: South Africa has already ratified the Protocol, and Zambia has not. In Zambia, where debate has been more limited, officials interviewed were largely ignorant of the Protocol and its content. Only a limited number of NGOs seemed sufficiently familiar with the African Women's Protocol to be able to use it to advance women's rights. With regard to Mozambique, the fact that the Protocol was adopted in Maputo did not seem to have had any significant effect on the levels of awareness among the general population. As in the other countries, very few people beyond those who had actually been directly involved in work on the Protocol knew anything about it. Promoting awareness about the Protocol must remain high on the agenda if it is to be an effective instrument of change.

Harnessing the force of the Protocol

The report identifies challenges but also focuses on case studies of good practice. These discuss ways of raising public awareness of the existence and use of international agreements; ways of creating a legal, policy, and institutional framework which enables women to realise their rights; and cases where international legal agreements have been used by women. A number of challenges must be faced in the process of harnessing the potential force of the African Women's Protocol. They include making good the gaps and weaknesses in the African Women's Protocol itself.

In common with most international human-rights instruments, the Protocol contains no sanctions for non-compliance. For monitoring, the African Women's Protocol relies on States to include a section on its implementation in their periodic reports on the implementation of the Charter. Yet these reports have not hitherto been very forthcoming. Given the poor record of compliance of States in fulfilling this obligation, advocates of women's rights will have to pressurise governments simultaneously on two fronts: first, with respect to the preparation of the report on implementation of the Charter, and second with regard to ensuring that it contains a meaningful report on the Protocol. It will be helpful for them to draw on CEDAW's experience of reporting processes, and devise measures such as NGO shadow reports and indicators to help to overcome weaknesses.

As regards implementation, there will be a need for a clear definition of the relationship between the Court and the

Commission, and the resolution of uncertainties with respect to competence. It is not yet clear how the merger of the Court on Human and People's Rights and the Court of Justice of the African Union will affect its capacity to promote and protect human rights. Countries will have to make a declaration accepting the competence of the Court to receive individual complaints before their citizens can enjoy this protection. In addition, unless adequate resources are provided, the Court will share the problems that the Commission experienced in its early years.

A key challenge is the absence of a culture that encourages the use of international human-rights instruments to realise all categories of human rights, including women's rights. The weakening of the women's movement in Africa in the past decade, and the weakness of key partnerships and alliances, are other hurdles that women must overcome. Lack of political will to address gender issues, and the weakness of policies and procedures intended to realise gender equality – in terms of power, resources, and skills – are some of the other challenges with which we must grapple. Other problems include the strength of patriarchy, tradition, culture, and religion; the co-existence of multiple legal systems; and the public/private dichotomy, which restricts women to the private sphere. Finally, there are threats in the wider political and economic context in which African women live their lives. These range from the diversion of resources to fund the international fight against terrorism, the implementation of economic policies which limit government spending on social services, and the rise in religious and cultural fundamentalisms. All these could roll back the gains made by women over the years.

Using the research to inform action
The report that came out of the research recommends the development of national/ regional plans or strategies which link actors, actions, and targets. The plans should include the following key elements:

- identification of champions (individuals) and key drivers (institutions) to lead the way;

- development of holistic national/ regional plans or strategies tailored to each country's/region's circumstances;

- development of tools for dissemination;

- support for activities to popularise the Protocol and ensure its ratification, domestication, and implementation;

- capacity building and efforts to strengthen vital or strategic organisations;

- meetings of key stakeholders, convened at national and regional levels to jump-start this process.

As we complete the research, we feel that a number of areas merit further research. They include the following.

- The implications of Article 17, on the right to participate in the determination of cultural policy. How best could this right be used to change women's lives? How does it relate to upholding women's rights in a context of cultural practices such as *lobola* (bride price), virginity testing, and initiation ceremonies? How does it relate to issues of sexuality?

- The situation with regard to the trafficking of women in southern Africa.

- The state of the women's movement in Africa in the twenty-first century, and the question of how it can be strengthened. In our view, this should include studies on the link between the growing numbers of women in public office and the status of women in general.

Since the research was undertaken, Oxfam has participated in a range of activities in relation to advocacy for women's rights and the African Women's Protocol in the southern African region.

Activities linked to World AIDS Day and the 16 days of activism

On 30 November 2004, at its offices in Pretoria, to mark the occasion of World AIDS Day and its intersection with the 16 Days of Activism Against Violence Against Women, Oxfam facilitated a Public Dialogue on the Protocol to the African Charter on Human and People's Rights on the Rights of Women in Africa. The focus of the event was on Sexual and Reproductive Health and HIV/AIDS, within the framework of the Women's Protocol.

Consultative workshops

Three consultative workshops were held to disseminate the findings of the policy research mentioned above to a range of actors, including academicians, parliamentarians, government officials, the African Union's Special Reporter on Women, the media, civil-society organisations, and Oxfam staff. The aim was to identify strategies for ratification, awareness raising, and domestic use of the Women's Protocol. The workshops included two national workshops, held in South Africa and Mozambique. There was an internal Oxfam workshop to develop the regional strategy and identify potential allies for popularising the Women's Protocol.

Regional strategy on the Africa Women's Protocol

Oxfam developed a regional strategy on the Protocol at a regional consultative workshop held in April 2005. The regional workshop aimed to disseminate the findings of the policy research to Oxfam country staff, and to identify elements that different sectors could incorporate into their programmes to further women's rights.

A draft regional strategy on the Protocol emerged, informed by the experiences of Oxfam staff and partner organisations of working with several institutions within the African Union; by our policy research on the Women's Protocol; and by some internal consultations with staff. The strategy lists activities that Oxfam will undertake at regional and country levels. We see the strategy as important not only in its own right, as a contribution to gender equality, but as an element in work to realise the Millennium Development Goals (MDGs) in Southern Africa.

Collaboration with the Pan African Parliament

In 2004 March, Oxfam's Pan Africa Policy Adviser and the Regional Gender Adviser for Oxfam in Southern Africa attended a launch of the Pan African Parliament in Addis Ababa. Since then, a coalition on African Women's Rights has been formed to raise public awareness and campaign for the ratification of the AU Women's Protocol across Africa. The coalition is composed of 19 organisations. Oxfam staff also attended the strategy workshop of the Gender, Family, Youth, and People with Disabilities Committee of the Pan African Parliament in April 2005. A draft strategy from this workshop is to be tabled in the fourth session of the Pan African Parliament, due in November 2005. The draft strategy identifies a number of areas which need attention if women's rights are to be realised.[4] As a way forward, the Oxfam GB Southern Africa region is to collaborate with the Gender, Family, Youth, and People with Disability Committee of the Pan African Parliament, sharing its experience with regard to HIV/AIDS.

In conclusion, our advocacy activities linked to the African Women's Protocol suggest to us that it is a potential force for positive change, despite its imperfections. The Protocol legitimises the struggles for gender equality and the promotion and protection of women's rights as an African struggle. If properly harnessed, it can serve as an effective tool to be used by African women, to support their empowerment.

This is an issue of fundamental human rights. In addition, empowering African women, who make up more than half of the continent's population, will have a positive multiplier effect, which will eventually produce happier, healthier, wealthier, and more harmonious families and societies.

Rose Gawaya has an MA degree in Development from the Institute of Social Studies in The Hague. She has worked for Oxfam GB since 2003 as the Regional Gender Advisor for Southern Africa. Before that she co-ordinated the Slum Aid Project in Uganda.

Notes

1 These are Comoros, Libya, Rwanda, Namibia, Djibouti, Cape Verde, Mali, Lesotho, Nigeria, South Africa, Senegal, and Malawi.

2 The methods used in the research were a literature review, interviews, and questionnaires. Key interviewees included officials of national governments and regional intergovernment organisations, parliamentarians and members of the Pan African Parliament, academics, and representatives of civil society and community-based organisations. A four-person team conducted the research. It included a lead researcher (Rosemary Semafumu Mukasa) and one national researcher per country.

3 The court's operationalisation has been delayed by a decision to merge it with the African Court of Justice. At the summit in Sirte, the Assembly of Heads of State decided that, pending consideration of a legal instrument to establish the merged court (which will be considered in the next session), all necessary measures for the functioning of the Human Rights Court (such as the election of judges, the determination of budgets, and the operationalisation of the registry) should proceed. No agreement was reached on the seat of the Court. If agreement is not reached between Tanzania and Mauritius, the two contenders, a vote will be taken next session.

4 These include fundraising; research; resource mobilisation; the development of a popular campaigning movement in Africa on HIV/AIDS, prostrate cancer, and maternal mortality; monitoring of individual countries' adoption and implementation of human-rights instruments; the strengthening of women's voices in decision making; and the promotion, ratification, in-country adoption, and implementation of the Africa Women's Protocol.

A voice of our own: advocacy by women with disability in Australia and the Pacific

Therese Sands, for People With Disability Australia Incorporated (PWDA)

Women with disability do not generally benefit from international human-rights laws and agreements, or from development discourse and practice. The interconnection between disability and gender identity is largely invisible within women's rights, disability rights, and development agendas. For women with disability in the Asia and Pacific region, this is particularly evident for Pacific women; within Australia, for Aboriginal and Torres Strait Islander women. This article discusses these issues in the context of PWDA's advocacy approach to disability, gender, and development. It also describes PWDA's engagement with women's human-rights projects, which has formed part of its advocacy strategy to develop a voice for Australian and Pacific women with disability.

People With Disability Australia Incorporated (PWDA) was founded in 1980, in the lead-up to the International Year of Disabled Persons (1981), to provide people with disability with a voice of their own. Our commitment to self-representation is reflected in our organisational structure: we are governed by a board of directors, all of whom are people with disability; the majority of employed staff are people with disability; and individuals with disability and organisations of people with disability are our primary voting membership. We have a cross-disability focus – that is, membership is open to people with all types of disability.

Our primary role is rights-based advocacy. We believe that disability, and gender and disability, need to become a priority and focus of development initiatives, aid programmes, poverty-alleviation strategies, and human-rights measures in Australia and the Pacific. We exercise our advocacy role locally and nationally within Australia, as well as regionally within the Pacific, and internationally. Our capacity-building work, in partnership with particularly disadvantaged population groups of people with disability, includes the development of advocacy skills to enable these groups to 'work the system' more effectively, to ensure that their needs are met and their rights respected within their own countries.

Disability and development in the Pacific

The World Health Organisation estimates that there are 600 million people with disability worldwide, with 80 per cent living in developing countries. People with disability in general, and women with disability in particular, are largely not recognised as a priority for development initiatives, aid programmes, poverty-alleviation strategies, and human-rights measures. Where they are identified as a specific target group, the focus is predominantly on rehabilitation, impairment prevention, health care, and the provision of technical aids and equipment – to the relative exclusion of strategies that would address underlying inequities, including gender inequity and the achievement of basic human rights. In addition, women with disability are invisible in measures that aim to progress gender equity and women's rights.

The largest number of people with disability, estimated at 400 million, lives in the Asia and Pacific region (UNESCAP 2005a). Pacific people with disability are at a particular disadvantage in the Asia and Pacific region, in relation to development, aid, and poverty-alleviation programmes. Pacific Island countries, with significantly smaller populations, usually living on small, geographically isolated islands, cannot compete with the high profile and visibility of the Asian region, which is the most populous region in the world.

Pacific people with disability, including Pacific women with disability, need to gain a higher profile in the Asia and the Pacific region. Donors and aid agencies, recipient governments, women's and human-rights organisations, and the Asia and Pacific region in general need to be persuaded of the significance of human-rights issues for people with disability. The development of a strong voice of people with disability is fundamental to this task of persuasion.

Our major capacity-building partnerships include working with Aboriginal and Torres Strait Islander people with disability, to develop their own self-representative organisation;[1] working with organisations of Pacific disabled people to develop a regional organisation of Pacific people with disability (the Pacific Disability Forum, or PDF); and supporting the activities of the Women with Disabilities Pasifika Network (WWDPN).[2]

The next part of this article will provide a discussion of the conceptual framework for PWDA's advocacy approach to disability, gender, and development.

Disability, gender, and development

While women's-rights activists and organisations have, to some extent, acknowledged the ways in which gender and race intersect each other to create particular locations of disadvantage for women, similar connections between gender and disability remain largely invisible. This means that the specific experience of women with disability remains essentially unacknowledged and unaddressed. Women with disability are themselves marginalised from women's organisations; everyday activities, such as meetings, consultations, information dissemination, support services and conferences, are often inaccessible to many women with disability. The policies, reports, advocacy projects, and development programmes that aim to address women's rights do not include, nor do they reach, women with disability.

This is particularly problematic in terms of development and aid that may be intended to help women to realise their human rights, but which in practice excludes women with disability from the benefits.

The interconnection between gender and disability also remains largely invisible in the work of disability-rights organisations. The way in which women experience disability is not generally acknowledged or explored. While everyday activities of these organisations may be accessible to women with disability, their specific issues as women are generally neither identified nor addressed in policies, reports, advocacy projects, and programmes aimed at achieving rights for people with disability.

Women with disability have responded to this exclusion by forming their own networks and organisations, such as WWDPN, and Women with Disabilities Australia.[3] Women with disability have succeeded to some extent in gaining recognition and having concerns addressed within disability organisations, such as PWDA. However, the interconnection between gender and disability is still largely unacknowledged in Community Based Rehabilitation (CBR), the predominant development practice that aims to address the rehabilitation needs of people with disability, in conjunction with equality of opportunity and social inclusion.

CBR has widespread support from disability and development organisations.[4] It is increasingly being seen as a development practice that needs to be linked to poverty-alleviation strategies, the Millennium Development Goals, and the achievement of human rights (UNESCAP 2005b). However, the issues and concerns of women with disability are not specifically identified in discussions concerning CBR, and nor is the question of involving women with disability as equal partners in CBR practice. CBR needs to be linked to development measures that address gender inequity and women's human rights, and it needs to develop measures to ensure that women with disability are active and equal partners.

Until the issues and concerns of women with disability are actively addressed within disability organisations and women's organisations and within development practice, women with disability will continue to be excluded from the human-rights and development gains made by women and will not achieve gender equity in relation to disability rights and development.

Key issues

It is very difficult to provide a definitive analysis of the status of women with disability. There is no comprehensive research, statistical analysis, or information that addresses how gender intersects with disability, and how gender, disability and poverty intersect. Women with disability have compiled the most comprehensive information about themselves. This information provides a global picture of exclusion, discrimination, poverty, violence, and human-rights abuse, which is based on the intersection between gender and disability, and gender, disability, and race.

Specific issues manifest themselves differently in each cultural, social, and political context, within countries and between countries, and in relation to specific types of impairment and condition. However, there is also significant agreement on the key issues identified by Australian and Pacific women with disability, as follows.[5]

Violence

Women with disability are at greater risk of all forms of violence than other women are. They are also less likely to be able to access support, refuge, or legal redress.

Violence against women with disability takes more forms than violence against other women. For example, Australian women with disability may experience violence in institutional settings, at the hands of personal care workers, and through forced sterilisation. In some Pacific Island communities, violence against women with disability is not considered a crime. In others, where there has been violent conflict and war, women with disability have been more likely to experience gender-based violence; and women are more likely to acquire disability as a result of gender-based violence.

Poverty

Women with disability are more likely to live on low incomes, and to experience absolute poverty, than other women. In our region, this is particularly the case for Aboriginal and Torres Strait Islander women with disability, and Pacific Island women with disability. The shameful level of poverty among Aboriginal and Torres Strait Islander people is also a major cause of disability, which is estimated to be at least twice that of the rest of the Australian population. In Pacific Island countries, poverty, and in some cases war and conflict, are major causes of disability.

Reproductive choice

Women with disability are commonly discouraged or prevented from having children, because they are widely perceived as being incapable of being mothers. In Australia, this may manifest itself as community disapproval of pregnant women with disability, forced sterilisation, children being taken from mothers judged to be 'unfit', and denial of reproductive technology. In Pacific Island countries, families often prevent women with disability from marrying and having a family.

Employment

Women with disability are more likely to be unemployed, or employed in the lowest-paid jobs, than men with disability and other women. Pacific Island women with disability are also unlikely to be able to access income-generation projects targeting women.

Education

Women with disability have fewer opportunities for education than men with disability and other women. Many Pacific Island and Aboriginal and Torres Strait Islander women with disability have no access to education.

Basic services

Women with disability in Australia are less likely to receive basic services, including disability, housing, and health services, than men with disability. They are often unable to access services specifically for women, such as breast screening and cervical screening. In many Aboriginal and Torres Strait Islander and Pacific Island communities, basic services are either absent or very limited.

Human rights and advocacy

About thirty years ago, the disability-rights movement conceptualised a social model of disability as a protest against the medicalised and professionalised discourses that prevailed at the time.[6] The social model of disability locates the problem of 'disability' within society. Society requires changing, in order for the human rights of people with disability to be realised. While an individual's functioning may be limited by impairments or health conditions, it is not these factors, but society, that disables people – by establishing and maintaining attitudinal, institutional, social, and environmental barriers that prevent access and inclusion within society. The individual and collective disadvantages faced by people with disability are located in a complex form of systemic discrimination that operates alongside, and intersects with, sexism, racism, and heterosexism. The social model is the basis from which many people with disability understand their oppression and campaign for the realisation of their human rights.

International human-rights instruments

The set of human-rights instruments commonly referred to as the International Bill of Rights[7] applies to people with disability as it does to any other person. In practice, however, people with disability have received very little benefit from the International Bill of Rights.

There are significant UN policy documents and action plans relating to disability,[8] but these do not have the higher status of conventions, which are legally binding on those governments that ratify them. Apart from the Standard Rules on the Equalisation of Opportunities for Persons with Disabilities (Standard Rules), these documents and action plans are outdated, and do not articulate or protect important human rights for people with disability.

In addition, only the Standard Rules specifically mention women with disability, largely as a result of lobbying and advocacy efforts by women with disability at the time when the Rules were being drafted (Sará-Serrano Mathiason 2003). However, the Rules deal with the issues and concerns of women with disability in only a limited way.

Apart from the Convention on the Rights of the Child, the thematic conventions that have been developed by the United Nations (UN) to articulate the particular needs and concerns of specific population groups do not specifically address or mention people with disability.[9] In addition, women with disability are not specifically mentioned in the Convention on the Elimination of All Forms of Discrimination Against Women (CEDAW).

CEDAW and the Beijing Platform for Action

Women with disability have been successful in lobbying the UN Committee that interprets and monitors CEDAW to adopt a General Recommendation on women with disability (Sará-Serrano Mathiason 2003). This General Recommendation on women with disability requires governments to provide information on women with disability in their periodic reports to the Committee, and in particular on measures that ensure equal access to education, employment, health services, and social security, and measures that ensure participation in all areas of social and cultural life.

However, although the General Recommendation has identified 'disability' as an issue within CEDAW, and governments to some extent now provide information about women with disability, the application of CEDAW to women with disability is largely *ad hoc*. CEDAW has provided women with disability with little practical protection and benefit.

The Beijing Platform for Action (BPFA) is a UN action plan that sets out actions in twelve critical areas on which governments need to focus, in order to make progress on realising the rights of women outlined in CEDAW. Unlike CEDAW, the BPFA does to some extent specifically mention issues for women with disability throughout the document. Again, women with disability were crucial to this inclusion, and their success depended on intensive lobbying throughout the development process of the draft Platform (Sará-Serrano Mathiason 2003).

While the BPFA does articulate some actions that are necessary for real progress towards the realisation of rights for women with disability, there has been limited implementation of these actions by individual governments. In addition, the BPFA is not legally binding. Women with disability do not have a convention that specifically and explicitly addresses their issues and concerns.

Disability Rights Convention

Only in 2001 did the United Nations agree to develop a thematic convention on the rights of people with disability. The development of the draft convention, 'Comprehensive and Integral International Convention on the Protection and Promotion of the Rights and Dignity of Persons with Disabilities' is currently underway, and the 6th United Nations Ad Hoc Committee Meeting took place in August 2005.

There are two key areas of debate that are extremely significant for Australian and Pacific women with disability: should the convention include the needs and concerns of specific population groups, including women with disability? And should the convention provide a framework for development and international co-operation?

There are arguments for and against specific recognition of women with disability in the convention. Some have argued against the inclusion of specific reference to women with disability because this may imply that it is the only article that is applied to this group; the other articles will not be seen as relevant to women with disability. A specific article may also imply that CEDAW does not apply to women with disability. Others have argued that the intersection of disability and gender creates greater disadvantage, and that, without specific reference and specific protections, women with disability will remain invisible and not benefit from the convention's implementation. This has been the experience of people with disability in all other conventions. Women with disability in Australia and the Pacific have stated their preference for a 'twin track' approach, where there is both specific reference to women with disability, and gender mainstreaming throughout the convention.[10]

In relation to the type of convention that should be developed, the debate focuses on arguments for a traditional convention on anti-discrimination and equality of opportunity, and arguments for a convention that recognises transfer of resources, knowledge, technical assistance, and policy advice to the developing world, where the majority of people with disability live.[11]

The outcome of these debates will have a significant influence on the question of whether the rights of women with disability will at last be explicitly articulated in international law and recognised in practice.

The Millennium Development Goals
Despite the interconnection between disability and poverty, the UN targets for global action against poverty – the Millennium Development Goals (MDGs) – are silent about people with disability. Yet the MDGs will be achieved only if poverty-alleviation measures take account of the needs and human rights of people with disability, including the specific issues and concerns of women with disability. The MDGs set a target for achieving gender equality, but this target is unlikely to be achieved for women with disability, if the basis of poverty and inequality for women with disability, the intersection of gender and disability, is not addressed.

Women worldwide have been critical of the extremely limited way in which gender equality is addressed and the failure to link the targets to CEDAW and BPFA.[12] The UN Development Fund for Women (UNIFEM) recommends that CEDAW and BPFA must be integrated with plans to achieve the MDGs, so that the MDGs can become a tool for implementation of CEDAW and the BPFA (UNIFEM 2005). However, given that women with disability have not felt the benefit of CEDAW or BPFA, this is unlikely to enhance application of the MDGs to women with disability.

In addition, Indigenous women in Australia are even more unlikely to benefit from the MDGs. It is not yet clear whether Australia will recognise the MDGs in relation to Indigenous communities, despite the fact that interconnection between disability and poverty in these communities is comparable to the situation in developing countries.

Biwako Millennium Framework
The *Biwako Millennium Framework for Action Towards an Inclusive, Barrier-Free and Rights-Based Society for Persons with Disabilities in Asia and the Pacific (BMF), 2003–2012* is the second regional UN action plan that sets targets to achieve rights for people with disability.

While gender issues were included to some extent in the first decade's Agenda for Action,[13] they were implemented in only a very limited way. By contrast, the BMF specifically identifies women with disability as the second of seven priority areas for action.

The BMF explicitly articulates the issues and concerns of women with disability, and recognises the intersection between gender and disability. Its main aim is to ensure that women with disability are fully included in self-help organisations of people with disability, in women's organisations, and in mainstream development initiatives, and that specific measures are adopted to safeguard their rights. A crucial action identified to achieve this is for governments, donors, disability organisations, and non-government organisations to build the capacity of women with disability to participate equally in policy, consultations, advocacy, and decision-making processes (UNESCAP 2002).

Overall, the BMF provides a strong framework for Australian and Pacific women with disability to demand and progress action that specifically targets protection of their rights, and in a way that stipulates their inclusion in the development and implementation of action.

The next section of this article describes PWDA's engagement with women's human-rights projects as part of its advocacy strategy to provide a voice for Australian and Pacific women with disability.

A voice of our own: from grassroots to global action

2004 and 2005 marked an important review period for three significant human-rights instruments for women:

- the twentieth anniversary of Australia's Sex Discrimination Act 1984;

- the NGO women's sector review of progress in implementing CEDAW, in preparation for the review of the Australian Government's report by the CEDAW Committee in January 2006; and

- the NGO women's sector preparations for the ten-year review of the Beijing Platform for Action (BPFA).

Two key processes were implemented to conduct these reviews:

- The Women's Report Card Project (WRCP). The NGO women's sector review of CEDAW is being driven by the Women's Rights Action Network Australia (WRANA), an unfunded network of women's rights activists. To date, this project has involved consultations with women in every

Australian State and Territory on the development of State and Territory reports on the status of women and, from these, the development of a National Community Report, 'Our Rights, Our Voices'.[14]

- The review to mark the twenty-year anniversary of the Commonwealth Sex Discrimination Act 1984 (SDA) and the ten-year review of BPFA were jointly driven by the Human Rights and Equal Opportunity Commission (HREOC), the government agency that administers the SDA, and two non-government organisations, the Centre for Refugee Research (CRR) and the Australian National Committee of Refugee Women (ANCORW). Three main activities were conducted within Australia as part of the review process: consultations with women throughout Australia, a Women's Human Rights Court, and a Women's Human Rights Workshop. The Court and Workshop were events for women in Australia and the Pacific, and were part of a range of events that were taking place throughout the world in preparation for the UN Commission on Status of Women (CSW) review of international implementation of BPFA.[15]

At PWDA we viewed these events as a significant opportunity for women with disability to have their voices heard, and to advocate for our issues and concerns to be integral to women's rights. It was also an opportunity to demonstrate that women with disability are significant advocates in the fight for women's rights.

The working groups responsible for planning and implementing the two review processes had a genuine commitment to ensuring that all women, in all their diversity, would be able to participate. While some working-group members had networks and experience in facilitating the participation of different groups of women, networks and experience in relation to women with disability were limited. A critical strategy was to ensure that PWDA was an active participant in the working groups, in order to provide expertise on disability and links with networks in the disability sector,[16] and to engage in advocacy on key issues.

Getting participation requirements 'right' for women with disability

A key issue was ensuring that participation requirements were recognised within the context of the social model of disability: meeting participation requirements is essential for the full inclusion of women with disability, and not an *ad hoc* or 'special' consideration.

PWDA provided expertise in planning activities, including asking invitees about their participation requirements, undertaking audits of venue access, booking sign-language interpreters, hiring hearing loops, providing accessible transport, and producing information in alternative formats, such as Braille and audio.

PWDA also needed to ensure that participation requirements were built into budgets at the planning stage. This became a significant issue when the funding body for one of the review processes allocated funds for specific activities, leaving no allocation for participation requirements. This meant that either some women with disability would not be able to participate, or additional funds must be obtained in order to facilitate their participation. On behalf of women with disability, PWDA decided to seek additional funding for sign-language interpreters, transport costs, and registration fees.

Inclusion of issues for women with disability

Another key challenge was ensuring that the issues and concerns of women with disability were explicitly represented in outcome documents and reports. On one occasion, PWDA was able to facilitate the development of a specific statement of recommendations by women with disability.[17]

However, it was also important for disability-related concerns to be included in the entirety of reports and within all issues, and not just within a reference to 'marginalised or vulnerable groups'. PWDA ensured that women with disability were part of the drafting of reports and recommendations and were able to provide comments on drafts. This not only produced beneficial outcomes for women with disability, but added significant value to outcome documents and reports by ensuring that they more accurately represent the views of women.

A significant challenge in relation to the Ten Year Review of the BPFA was the impossibility of engaging in direct advocacy about issues for women with disability during the Asian and Pacific NGO women's meeting, and the CSW meeting that followed the Australian events. Without funds, it was difficult to maintain a physical presence of women with disability, and this affected the degree to which issues for women with disability were included in the Asia and Pacific lobbying document that was used during the CSW. As a response to this problem, PWDA developed a 'call to action' lobbying statement, which was distributed by the Australian NGO delegation to other NGO and government delegations during the CSW review process.[18] We also liaised with the Chair of the Women's Committee of Disabled Peoples' International to support her presence on behalf of women with disability during the CSW review process.[19]

Countering invisibility

An essential advocacy strategy to counter the invisibility of women with disability in women's-rights organisations and activities was to ensure that women with disability were involved in all activities in the review processes. PWDA organised women with disability to participate and contribute: as participants in consultations, as speakers, as specialist human-rights commentators, workshop organisers and facilitators, as scribes, as trainers, and as report writers.

To challenge any concept of women with disability as a homogeneous group, and to ensure representation of the views of women with disability, it was crucial for the diversity of women with disability to be visible. This meant ensuring that there was representation of women with a range of impairments and conditions, from a range of backgrounds and identities: women with disability from diverse cultural and linguistic backgrounds, Indigenous women with disability, lesbians with disability, mothers with disability, young women with disability, and older women with disability.

Ensuring inclusion within the region

Pacific women with disability are usually excluded from important women's events and forums in the Asia and Pacific region, despite the fact that these events affect their daily lives and their ability to realise their rights. In the Pacific sub-region, Australia and New Zealand are the usual dominant voices.

Representation and participation of the Women with Disabilities Pasifika Network was essential to providing a unique voice for Pacific women at the events held for Australian and Pacific women – the Women's Human Rights Court and Workshop. Through the Global Fund for Women, PWDA sponsored two women with disability to participate, one from Fiji and one from Solomon Islands. These events provided an opportunity for Pacific women with disability to tell their stories to the assembly at the Women's Human Rights Court, to raise their issues during Workshop sessions, to network with other Pacific, Australian, and Aboriginal women, and to meet with donors and human-rights organisations.

Major outcomes

There were major positive outcomes from engaging in these projects. Women with disability had a strong, active presence in all aspects of consultation and workshop events. Women with disability commented on the importance of being part of these events: they were able to learn about women's rights, discuss the relationship between disability rights and women's rights, and develop networks with women's rights and donor organisations. Participants and organisers learned about facilitating the participation of women with disability, about disability issues, and the intersection between gender and disability. Many participants and organisers commented on the strong participation of women with disability, how their contribution added value to outcomes, and the on-going value of developing and maintaining networks with women with disability. The workshop events provided an opportunity for WWDPN and Aboriginal women with disability to talk directly to development and human-rights agencies about the issues and concerns of Pacific women with disability and Aboriginal women with disability.

The contribution and participation of women with disability are reflected in, and add value to, the documents, media releases, reports, and statements which came from the projects. The inclusion of women with disability reflects the true diversity of women, and the inclusion of this diversity strengthens the project process and the content of outcome documents and reports. In addition, women with disability can use the documents, reports, and statements as advocacy tools. The participation of WWDPN was significant not only because it provided a unique voice for Pacific women with disability, but also because it conveyed a strong sense of unity among women with disability in the region. It demonstrated that women with disability will not be marginalised or excluded from mainstream women's events, and that women with disability are key contributors to activism for women's rights.

Conclusion: future directions

For us Australian and Pacific women with disability, developing a strong voice is essential to having our needs and concerns identified and addressed on agendas relating to disability rights, women's rights, and development.

There are key actions that still need to be taken to achieve this. We need in-country human-rights training, leadership and skills development for women with disability, and the formation of self-help networks of women with disability. Capacity building is required for self-help networks of Pacific women with disability to ensure that women with disability achieve political recognition of their concerns at both national and regional levels. Australian and Pacific women with disability need to be fully and equally included in the decision making and management of organisations of people with disability and in women's-rights organisations. Alliances need to be forged with disability, women's, and development agencies, with Australian and Pacific women with disability continuing to develop and implement mutually supportive advocacy strategies.

The profile and visibility of Pacific people with disability need to be raised with development and donor agencies. The development strategies of development and donor agencies must prioritise people with disability, including women with disability, and Aboriginal and Torres Islander people with disability. Development and donor agencies need to implement human-rights approaches to disability, gender, and development: approaches which are inclusive of people with disability, including women with disability. They should also align development policies and practices in the Pacific with the BMF. Australian and Pacific women with disability must continue to contribute to debates about gender equity and the inclusion of women with disability in the development of the draft convention.

A significant challenge in progressing these issues is the on-going effort, resources, and funding required by consistent engagement in three arenas: women's rights, disability rights, and development practice. In relation to women's rights and development practice, initial advocacy efforts can often be consumed by the struggle to have participation requirements met. In the disability-rights arena, it is necessary to constantly profile the gender-specific aspects of issues. In all three arenas, women with disability have to ensure that they are recognised as women first and rights bearers. While similar strategies may be used to profile issues and concerns of women with disability within these arenas, considerable work is required to build knowledge and networks, establish credibility, and understand concepts and systems specific to each arena.

However, the benefits of this advocacy work are significant: creating a synergy between women's rights, disability rights, and development practice where women with disability achieve visibility, equity, and full inclusion. Along with other women and men with disability, women with disability will also benefit from human-rights law and practice and development discourse and practice.

Therese Sands is a Senior Advocate for People With Disability Australia Incorporated, with a particular focus on building the capacity of Australian and Pacific women with disability to participate in and benefit from human-rights and development discourse and practice. Address: PWDA, PO Box 666, Strawberry Hills NSW 2012, Australia.
Email: tsands@pwd.org.au
Website: www.pwd.org.au

Notes

1 Aboriginal and Torres Strait Islander people are the Indigenous people of Australia. The Aboriginal Disability Network was formed in the Australian State of New South Wales in December 2002.

2 WWDPN was formed in December 2003. Its current members are women with disability from Australia, Cook Islands, Fiji, Kiribati, Nauru, New Zealand, Papua New Guinea, Solomon Islands, Samoa, and Vanuatu.

3 Women with Disabilities Australia (WWDA) is the peak organisation for women with all types of disabilities in Australia. It is the only organisation of its kind in Australia, and one of only a few around the world.

4 For example, Disabled Peoples' International (DPI) and the International Disability and Development Consortium (IDDC), which is a consortium of 15 international NGOs involved in disability and development work.

5 These key issues have been gathered from consultations and formal and informal meetings that PWDA has facilitated and/or attended with Australian and Pacific women with disability. Comprehensive information on Australian women with disability is available on the website of Women with Disabilities Australia at www.wwda.org.au

6 For a history of the origins of the social model of disability, see the website of Disability Awareness in Action at www.daa.org.uk/social_model.html

7 The International Bill of Rights is made up of the Universal Declaration of Human Rights, the International Covenant on Civil and Political Rights, and the International Covenant on Economic, Social and Cultural Rights.

8 These include the Declaration on the Rights of Mentally Retarded Persons (1971), the Declaration on the Rights of Disabled Persons (1975), the World Program of Action Concerning Disabled Persons (1982), the Principles for the Protection of Persons with Mental Illness and the Improvement of Mental Health Care (1991), and the Standard Rules on the Equalisation of Opportunities for Persons with Disabilities (1993).

9 The thematic conventions developed to date are the Convention relating to the Status of Refugees, Convention on the Elimination of All Forms of Racial Discrimination (CERD), the Convention on the Elimination of All Forms of Discrimination Against Women (CEDAW), the Convention on the Rights of the Child (CRC), and the International Convention on the Protection of the Rights of All Migrant Workers and Members of Their Families.

10 This position has been expressed within two statements of recommendations, 'Statement by women with disability from the Pacific sub-region' and 'Women with Disabilities Pasifika Network Tanoa Statement', which concluded events for women with disability in 2004. PWDA's position on the inclusion of women with disability was most recently expressed during the 6th UN Ad Hoc Committee Meeting held in New York in August 2005. The statements and PWDA's position are on PWDA's website at www.pwd.org.au/international_news.html

11 At the 6th UN Ad Hoc Committee Meeting, PWDA and Disability Promotion and Advocacy Association, Vanuatu jointly made an intervention stating their argument for a convention that specifically addresses the right to development and international cooperation. This intervention is on PWDA's website at www.pwd.org.au/disabilityconvention/index.html

12 For a comprehensive gender analysis of the MDGs, see *Gender and Development* Volume 13, number 1, March 2005.

13 The Agenda for Action for the Asian and Pacific Decade of Disabled Persons, 1993–2002.

14 Available on the WRANA website at http://home.vicnet.net.au/~wrana/ The next stage of this project will involve the development of an alternative, Shadow Report to the Government's report, and preparations for the UN CEDAW Committee review of the Australian Government in January 2006. .

15 A key outcome of the three events was the development of a document, 'Women Taking Action Locally and Globally', which was used to feed into the Asian and Pacific women's lobbying document prepared for the CSW event. The outcomes document is available on the Centre for Refugee Research at www.crr.unsw.edu.au/beijing+10.html

16 In particular, Women with Disabilities Australia (WWDA), the NSW Network of Women with Disabilities, and the Women with Disabilities Pasifika Network.

17 The 'Statement by Women with Disability from the Pacific sub-region' is available on PWDA's website at www.pwd.org.au/publications/womens_statement.html

18 'Women and girls with disability – A Call to Action' is available on PWDA's website at www.pwd.org.au/publications/csw.html

19 The position paper developed by Disabled Peoples' International can be viewed online at www.whrnet.org/docs/issue-position_disabilities.html. The Chair of the Women's Committee was also interviewed by the Association for Women's Rights in Development. The interview is available online at www.whrnet.org/docs/interview-radtke-0503.html

References

Elwan, Anne (1999) 'Poverty and Disability: A Survey of the Literature', Social Protection Discussion Paper No. 9932, World Bank, http://siteresources.worldbank.org/DISABILITY/Resources/Poverty/Poverty_and_Disability_A_Survey_of_the_Literature.pdf (last checked by the author August 2005).

Sará-Serrano Mathiason, Maria-Cristina (2003) 'Women with Disabilities: Lessons of Reinforcing the Gender Perspective in International Norms and Standards', www.un.org/esa/socdev/enable/women/wwdis0.htm (last checked by the author August 2005).

United Nations Development Fund for Women (UNIFEM) (2005) 'Pathway to Gender Equality: CEDAW, Beijing and the MDGs', www.unifem.org/filesconfirmed/216/385_pathwaytogenderequality_screen.pdf (last checked by the author August 2005).

United Nations Economic and Social Commission for Asia and the Pacific (UNESCAP) (2002) 'Biwako Millennium Framework', www.unescap.org/esid/psis/disability/bmf/bmf.html#Targets (last checked by author August 2005).

United Nations Economic and Social Commission for Asia and the Pacific (UNESCAP) (2005a) 'Disability Programme', www.unescap.org/esid/psis/disability/index.asp (last checked by author August 2005).

United Nations Economic and Social Commission for Asia and the Pacific (UNESCAP) (2005b) 'UNESCAP Workshop on Community-Based Rehabilitation (CBR) and Poverty Alleviation of Persons with Disabilities', Bangkok: UNESCAP.

Advocacy for an end to poverty, inequality, and insecurity: feminist social movements in Pakistan

Khawar Mumtaz

In this paper, taken from a presentation given to the Women In Development Europe (WIDE) Conference 2005, I consider the situation in Pakistan, within the general context of South Asia as a whole, and focus on the questions that confront feminists today. These questions, I believe, may be relevant to women activists not only in the South but also elsewhere. I discuss the activities of feminists who are engaging in advocacy for gender equality in Pakistan. This is an uphill task, but it has nevertheless resulted in some achievements. Not least of these is Pakistani women's success in bringing women's rights to the attention of both policy makers and the general public.

To be a feminist is to be in a continuous state of reflection and learning. Looking back at the past hundred years or so of South Asia's history, I would argue that feminist movements have played a constant part in this history. They have changed over time, depending on the demands of their various contexts, and they are constantly being redefined and rejuvenated today.

Shaped by the nature and content of the wider struggle for independence from colonial rule, Pakistani women's articulation of their rights has taken a variety of forms. It was possible, from the early years of the twentieth century, for women to demand the right to education; to agitate for the right to inheritance and an end to polygamy; and to lobby for voting rights, as the struggle for independence gained momentum. The campaign for Pakistani autonomy gained pace in 1946–47, demanding a separate state for Muslims in the Indian sub-continent when it gained independence from British rule. The movement saw a mass mobilisation of Muslim women who had never before stepped out of their homes (Mumtaz and Shaheed 1987).

However, located within the framework of the larger struggle for national sovereignty, women's struggles tended to fade from prominence when the objectives of the principal struggle were achieved. Subsequently, however, came events that triggered the re-emergence of women's demands for the realisation of their rights: in Bangladesh, political upheaval; in Sri Lanka, insurgency; in Pakistan, repressive government action; and internationally, events such as the United Nations series of conferences on women, running from 1975 to 1995, and the related activities of the international women's movements.

For women's movements in different parts of South Asia, a turning point arrived when they became autonomous, or strove to be so. I am referring to autonomy from political parties, local pressure groups, and official or government influence. In a way, the 1970s and 1980s marked the arrival of the feminist movement in South Asia. Influenced to some extent by the thinking of the women's movements in the West, it manifested itself in Pakistan as a platform (the Women's Action Forum, formed to oppose the *Hudood* Ordinances, which are discussed in the next section), and as dispersed groups demanding an end to dowry deaths (in India), or denouncing violence or demanding land rights (in India and in other parts of the region). What defined this coming of age was the assertion of women's identity, needs, and aspirations, and the de-linking of activism to promote women's rights from the activism of organisations which advocate political rights, the rights of workers, and so on.

In the next section, I focus on the experience of the women's movement in Pakistan specifically.

The Pakistan experience

The contemporary women's movement in Pakistan dates back to the early 1980s, when its head of state, General Zia-ul Haq, used religion to legitimise his rule and colluded with religious forces. He promulgated, among other measures, the *Hudood* Ordinances (1979).[1] These constitute the most pernicious and discriminatory piece of legislation that Pakistani women have ever seen. It has had far-reaching and devastating consequences, particularly for poor women. It makes no distinction between adultery (sexual activity outside marriage undertaken with the consent of the woman) and rape (violation of a woman through forced sex). It affects the ways in which courts work, in that it excludes the evidence of women and religious minorities, and provides for stoning to death and flogging if *Hadd* (maximum violation under the law) is proved.

It was the first conviction under this law that galvanised urban professional women, and women's organisations, to form the Women's Action Forum (WAF). As WAF protested, demonstrated, and publicly challenged the laws and other forms of discrimination against women in Pakistan, it vigorously defended its autonomy, distancing itself from political parties, trade unions, and professional associations. Equally vigorously, it defined its struggle as a struggle against the martial-law regime, and for democracy.

For almost ten years, WAF represented Pakistani women's voice and resistance. In this period, it succeeded in putting women's issues on the agenda. No political party manifesto was complete without mentioning women's rights, and public discourse about women's unequal status in society was articulated in and beyond the media. This discourse focused on issues that included women's rights to work and to participate in political life; the division drawn by customary practices (and condoned by the State) between public and private spaces; and its impact on women. It also focused on the particular concerns of women heads of households. The volume of research on women by women increased very significantly. Issues that were formerly taboo, such as rape, killing in the name of honour, violence against women, and harmful customs, were brought into the public domain.

By 1988, democracy had been restored in Pakistan, elections held, and a woman prime minister (Benazir Bhutto) elected. The women's movement seemed to lose its steam, and the passion and anger that had driven it became diffused. In the following decade, women's development organisations were established. Funds became available. A new strategy evolved: that of influencing government and policy makers through engagement and dialogue. Women activists were now members of advisory committees and working groups, and they wrote policy papers and reports. Advocacy continued in this new form – working with parliamentarians and politicians, and through the media. Feminists made international alliances, through UN conferences and global networks.

The decade of the 1990s saw Pakistan in political turmoil, struggling under a heavy burden of external debt, forced to adopt economic structural adjustment policies,[2] and facing the rise of religious extremists, who were tolerated and mollified by successive governments. This was the period of growing xenophobia, intolerance on the basis of ethnic differences, persecution of minorities and development organisations, the use of the gun to settle scores, and the visible induction of women into 'fundamentalist' parties and groups. The antagonism of politico-religious men against women sharpened, as women's organisations reached out to poor women in rural areas, persuading them to cast votes or to go to school.

In this context, from the mid-1990s onwards, the women's movement became a part of the movement for civil liberties and minority rights; of the anti-nuclear movement (after the testing of nuclear devices by India and Pakistan); of the anti-dam and pro-environment movement (in the wake of the government's intention to build large new dams, and the emergence of the suffering of those displaced by dams constructed earlier in Tarbela and Mangla); and the peace movement (following military clashes and tensions with India). Similar developments could be seen in India: for example, the anti-Narmada Dam movement, and the protests after the Gujarat mass killings in 2002 (Ahmed 2004). Other social movements that emerged in Pakistan in this period involved the active participation of women in confrontations with police and paramilitary forces. The formation of the peasant movement in the Punjab was triggered in 2000 with the announcement that the status of peasants working on army-controlled lands was being changed from that of tenant farmers to that of lessees, tilling the land on contract. The move would deprive them of rights under the tenancy laws and make them vulnerable to eviction from the lands that their families had cultivated for more than one hundred years.[3] These movements received active support from feminists and human-rights activists.

The big challenge from the mid-1990s (as in the previous era before the 1980s, when women's rights became an issue in themselves) has been to locate campaigns for women's rights within the broader struggle, and to ensure that women are included in decision-making processes. However, in my view the feminist movement, in opting to close ranks with movements for social justice, has not done so at the cost of its own autonomy. This has been possible through the process, initiated in the mid-1970s (by a relatively small group of women), of addressing women's issues on their own merit, rather than as part of the agenda of existing organisations promoting women's social welfare, or political parties, or labour or peasant groups. In the 1980s, when political parties and activities were banned in Pakistan, women established their autonomy by being the first to publicly challenge the military government of the day. It is a measure of the steadfastness of the feminists in maintaining their political positions that the space that they carved for themselves then has been respected, as well as maintained.

In the next section I review the progress made towards realising women's rights in Pakistan, and consider questions to inform future directions.

Reviewing our progress and asking some questions

Women in Pakistan have made some significant gains in their campaigns to realise their human rights over the past three decades. CEDAW has been ratified. Thirty-three per cent of seats are reserved for women in local government bodies, and 17 per cent are similarly reserved in parliament. This breakthrough came in 2000, after relentless, decade-long campaigning. There is a 5 per cent quota for women in government jobs. The government is making greater allocations of its budget for women's programmes: for instance, for the period 2005–2010, Pakistan Rupees 4.1 billion have been earmarked to fund activities designed to improve women's social, economic, and political empowerment through existing programmes and new initiatives, including technical skills training, micro-finance schemes, rehabilitation and protection centres for women in distress, and institutional reforms.[4]

In addition, there is greater visibility of women in the electronic media. There is recognition of the phenomenon of 'honour' killing as needing legislation by the government and political parties (although the Honour Killing Law passed by Parliament in 2005 fell short of women activists' expectations, by not taking into account conflict with other laws that makes the new legislation ineffective). A permanent National Commission on the Status of Women has been established. In 2002, a National Policy for Women's Development and Empowerment was announced.

Finally, the *Hudood* Ordinances have been undergoing review since 2003, for repeal or amendment. As stated earlier, the *Hudood* Ordinances have been a major focus of women's advocacy and agitation for their repeal since the formation of WAF in 1981. The persistence with which women activists took up specific cases of women's victimisation under the law, researched the abuse of the law, and drew attention to the manifold multiplication of women in prison since the promulgation of the *Hudood* laws finally led the Senate to establish a Commission of Inquiry for Women in 1997. The Commission, reviewing all laws and their impact on women, upheld the position of women activists and recommended the repeal of the law.

In the face of the government's reluctance to adopt the Commission's report (primarily because of the religious lobby's support of the law as being 'Islamic'), the agitation and advocacy continued relentlessly. Finally, the occurrence of yet another case of victimisation of a woman under the law compelled the National Commission on the Status of Women, headed by a retired woman judge, to undertake once again in 2003 the task of reviewing the law and its impact on women. The Commission unanimously recommended the repeal of the Ordinances. This was followed by the official decision to review the law for amendment or repeal.

Yet despite these successes, much remains to be done. The ratio of women to men in Pakistan remains seriously distorted in men's favour, at 108:100, reflecting bias against women which results in the deaths of female foetuses, girl children, and adult women. Between 350 and 500 women out of 100,000 die in childbirth (Mumtaz 2004); there is a 30 per cent gap in male:female primary-school enrolment; domestic violence and violence against women are rampant; and – a cause for very serious concern – the majority of women do not know their rights and are not aware of the existence of the women's movement.

South Asia currently remains mired in conflict arising from religion, class, and ethnicity, as well as cross-border conflicts. Democratic systems have not taken root in the region; despite regular elections in some countries, most of the states are over-developed and autocratic, and violence is rampant. The states are under pressure from the forces of economic globalisation and pressure to privatise. Governments are withdrawing from their responsibilities to provide basic services to citizens, in line with the requirements of international financial institutions. In Pakistan, poverty, insecurity, and inequality are deepening (Government of Pakistan 2003): more than one third of the population is living below the poverty line. High levels of national debt have reduced the autonomy of decision makers. The international 'war on terror' has strengthened the resolve of political–religious groups to accelerate their campaign against the West and against the government, which they see as bowing down to external pressures, and this has led to greater repression and reduction of opportunities for secular politics. Growing numbers of citizens are joining extremist groups. Increased religious extremism and intolerance fuel rising violence, and threaten women's rights. The women's movement is, on the one hand, opposed in principle to the military government and its repressive policies, and is at the same time strongly opposed to obscurantist official policies regarding the form of government, women's role in society, and the government's support of religious extremists.

There is a perspective that regards all struggles as women's struggles, and there is general agreement among women activists in Pakistan that this is indeed the case; only by being a part of these other struggles can we ensure that those in power pay heed to women's voices and perspectives. The premise still holds that various social movements have given women the space to agitate for their rights. However, since they established their movement as autonomous in the 1990s, the challenge for feminists is to define their own agendas and forms of struggle, rather than waiting for opportunities that arise externally. It is therefore imperative to build alliances with those struggling for social justice; to get involved in international processes and global movements; to fine-tune a multiple-pronged strategy of (on the one hand) challenging measures that push women into greater poverty and insecurity and (on the other hand) using every opportunity of influencing government, corporations, and donors to bring accountability and transparency in politics and democracy; and to help women discover their own agency.

Conclusion – some questions

There are differences among feminists regarding the strategies that we need to use when working in partnership with others to campaign for the rights of women. Some of these are enormous global questions. How do we change patriarchal norms that perpetuate male domination? How do we arrest the current return to narrow, restrictive, and fundamentalist beliefs which reverse the gains made? How do we ensure that the World Social Forum,[5] and other important social movements challenging economic globalisation, take on the issue of gender equality and women's concerns?

More immediate, locally focused dilemmas include (among many others) the following questions.

How do we challenge prejudiced perceptions of feminists?

The critique of the women's rights movement in Pakistan has centred on the urban, middle-class identity of feminists, and on perceptions that these women are westernised, fail to respect customs and traditions, and lead younger women astray.

This caricature is the opposite of the commonly held notion of shy, voiceless, 'covered' women, who need male protection. It is true that some feminists sport short hair, and most of them are professional working women, who are outspoken and independent of men. It is also true that they do not dress in *purdah* or *hijab,* and that they challenge patriarchal norms and demand equality. These characteristics lead to the label of 'westernised'. It is urbanised, middle-class women who are in a position to take the risks associated with challenging gender norms, protected as they are by their class and by their comparatively greater knowledge of social institutions and systems, and how to access resources. Women living in poverty, even those desiring changes in gender relations, can frequently neither spare the time from their burdened daily existence nor risk the consequences of taking public action to advance their collective interests.

Interestingly, such caricaturing of feminists is done by the media, by religious groups and right-wing political groups, and at times by government itself, rather than by women living in poverty.

How can we use and subvert established systems, without getting co-opted?

One key issue on which differing opinions exist among feminists is the danger of co-option by other parties, particularly the government. Activists have debated the nature of the ideal kind of engagement with the government, and the ways in which women should engage in dialogue and participate in activities and tasks instigated by government. Another form of co-option may take place if women's organisations accept funds from donors for advocacy and capacity-building activities.

How, too, should we engage with actors who hold opinions with which we radically disagree? An example would be women politicians who belong to religious political parties and rabidly oppose feminists and activists for women's rights. In some contexts, it may seem to be a lesser evil to engage than to refuse to engage. For example, should women's organisations become involved in facilitating women's participation in local elections under laws enacted by a military government?

How can we achieve a widespread impact?

Finally, we have needed to consider how we should continue our work in a context in which much needs to be done, but there are never sufficient numbers of us to do it. How will we sustain energy in our campaigning for women's rights in Pakistan, bearing in mind the fact that we have not been able to attract many younger women into the fold? And how far should we spread our energies? Throughout the years of UN processes in support of women's rights, we have spent much time and energy on advocacy and related activities. Has it been worth it, and what is the cost of having decided to invest time in this way? As Pakistani women activists, can we afford to remain out of the international arena? Women's organisations in Pakistan have in a way informally divided the work and responsibilities among themselves. Some have linked themselves to global processes and some to regional processes, and others have chosen to work within Pakistan. There is a growing realisation that we cannot de-link ourselves from global advocacy processes and debates, because they have far-reaching implications for our lives. It is critically important in this context to share global experiences and link international learning on women's lives with our in-country realities and analyses.

Khawar Mumtaz is Co-ordinator of Shirkat Gah Women's Resource Centre, 68 Tipu Block, New Garden Town, Lahore, Pakistan. E-mail: khawar@sgah.org.pk.

Notes

1 The *Hudood* Ordinances 1979 are a composite of five laws dealing with adultery, theft, bodily harm, consumption of illegal drugs and alcohol, and the giving of false evidence. Their promulgation was the trigger for the formation of WAF. For details, see Mumtaz and Shaheed 1987, and Asma Jahangir and Hina Jilani, *The Hudood Ordinances: A Divine Sanction*, Lahore: Rohtas Books, 1990.

2 Structural Adjustment Programmes are part of the IMF's conditions for giving loans to developing countries. States are required to open up to foreign trade, attract foreign investments, remove subsidies, impose additional taxes, deregulate laws, and downsize enforcement agencies. As a result, in most countries that are subject to SAPs, indigenous industry is forced out of the market because it is unable to compete

with multinational companies; privatisation of social services – usually unaffordable for the poor – is introduced; emphasis is placed on encouraging exports, at the expense of the food requirements of the majority; and the poor become poorer. For details in the context of Pakistan, see T.J. Banuri, S.R. Khan, and M. Mahmood (eds.) *Just Development; Beyond Adjustment with a Human Face*, Karachi: Oxford University Press, 1997; and N. Sadeque, *Debt by Entrapment*, Karachi: Shirkat Gah, 2001.

3 For more details, see Samiya Mumtaz: 'Masters, not friends', *Newsline*, November 2002, pp. 84-92.

4 Figures from page 170, *Mid Term Development Framework 2005–2010*, Planning Commission, Government of Pakistan, Islamabad: Government of Pakistan, 2005.

5 The World Social Forum is the platform that came into being as a counterpoint to the World Economic Forum, held annually in Davos. 2005 is the fifth year of the WSF. Initially held in Porto Alegre, Brazil, the WSF was held in India in 2004.

References

Ahmed, S. (2004) 'Sustaining peace, re-building livelihoods: the Gujarat Livelihoods Project', *Gender and Development*, 12 /3: 94-102.

Government of Pakistan (2003) *Poverty Reduction Strategy Paper*, Karachi: Government of Pakistan.

Mumtaz, K. (2004) *Cairo Ten Years On*, Karachi: Shirkat Gah.

Mumtaz, K. and F. Shaheed (1987) *Women of Pakistan: Two Steps Forward, One Step Back?* London: Zed Books.

Advocacy training by the International Community of Women Living with HIV/AIDS

Emma Bell

The International Community of Women Living with HIV/AIDS joined forces with the POLICY project with the aim of developing an advocacy agenda on sexual and reproductive health rights, and access to care, treatment, and support for women living with HIV/AIDS in South Africa and Swaziland. The process began with an assessment of the concerns and experiences of HIV-positive women, and the policy and institutional environment. A workshop was subsequently held in Durban, involving 45 HIV-positive women from Swaziland and South Africa, to discuss the assessment and identify priority issues for advocacy. The same group of women met two months later and produced a plan which directly addresses the reality of HIV-positive women's lives.

The International Community of Women Living with HIV/AIDS (ICW) is the only international network of HIV-positive women. Our members, in 134 countries, work with local, national, and international networks, organisations, and groups supporting and campaigning for the rights of HIV-positive women and men.

ICW was established in 1992 in response to the desperate lack of support, information, and services available worldwide to women living with HIV, and to enable these women to influence and contribute to official policy development. HIV-positive women from around the world attended the eighth International Conference on AIDS, held in Amsterdam in July 1992, where they shared stories and strategies for coping. They also devised action plans for the future. Because they did not want to lose the momentum created at the conference, ICW came into being. Our vision for ourselves and for all HIV-positive women is to create a world

- in which we are involved in a respected and meaningful way in decision making which affects our lives, at all political levels;

- in which we have access to full care and treatment, regardless of our age or lifestyle;

- in which all our economic, social, and political rights are respected, including our right to make choices concerning our sexual and reproductive lives, and our right to live free of discrimination in all areas of our lives, irrespective of our culture, age, religion, sexuality, social or economic status or class, and race.

At ICW, we believe that the second and third aspects of this vision will not be realised in the absence of the first. This is why ICW members around the world can be found advocating not merely for involvement, but for meaningful involvement, in decisions that affect our lives. Sadly, legal and policy changes are too often determined by people who do not understand the realities in which HIV-positive women live their lives. Our members know what it is to live with HIV, and they know what they need in order to improve their well-being, yet others continue to speak on our behalf or judge us. For women and men living with HIV and AIDS, meaningful participation in policy making and reporting on the impact of existing policies continues to be the exception rather than the rule. When it does occur, it tends to be tokenistic. We feel that, without greater – and better-integrated – political participation by HIV-positive women, we will not achieve the support that we need. As long as we are not the ones determining the direction of policies and programmes, genuine and positive change is unlikely to happen.

Factors that prevent women's participation in decision making

In this section, I discuss some factors which limit the involvement of HIV-positive women in decision-making processes.

Negative attitudes

The following quotations illustrate the exclusion of HIV-positive women from forums where policies and decisions are made. (Like all quotations presented in this article, these come from workshops conducted in 2005 by ICW in Lesotho, Swaziland, and South Africa as part of a wider advocacy-focused project.)

- 'We are always submissive and do not challenge those in authority.'

- 'When you voice your idea, your idea is not accepted because of your status.'

- 'Our input is not implemented, and our ideas are not taken into consideration.'

- 'Men that are decision makers feel that women's place is in the kitchen.

We don't feel part of the decision-making community.'

- 'We have organisations, but men lead them, and our issues don't get discussed.'

- 'Policymakers sit in board rooms and decide what is relevant to our lives – we are not part of the process.'

The marginalisation of HIV-positive women is not only a feature of mainstream policy arenas. National and international HIV organisations and networks should be a source of support for HIV-positive women, and should involve them fully in decision making. However, they often reflect the gender discrimination that is found in society more generally. Despite women's strong presence in support groups, national (and international) groups of people living with HIV/AIDS are dominated by men. *'There is always a male AIDS activist responding to programmes on the TV and radio about HIV-positive women and pregnancy. An AIDS activist on the radio was asked about HIV-positive women having babies. He doesn't feel it is their right, yet he has two children'* (ICW Rapid Assessment, South Africa 2005).

Practical issues

HIV-positive women are often overburdened with caring for others and bringing up children, as well as looking after their own health. Our members report that care and support for people infected or affected by HIV and AIDS is carried out almost exclusively by people (especially women) who are themselves infected or affected. Positive women are active in health-care settings, as counsellors, in home-based care, and in community education through churches, schools, and other community groups; they are often very active in setting up and administering support groups, and in providing for orphans and other vulnerable children, and for elderly people. Nearly all such work is done on a voluntary basis, without strong external support or official recognition, despite the fact that it is effectively supplementing the inadequate services that are available from governments and NGOs. Governments worldwide fail to provide the level of services that is required by people living with HIV and AIDS.

Alliances could be built between carers and service providers (actual and potential), and carers could be consulted about future policy and programming. There is plenty happening at the community level that could be used to influence policy or programme formulation, but no one is asking women 'What is the right thing to do?'. Furthermore, women living with HIV and AIDS are so busy providing community-level care and supporting service-delivery activities that they lack time and resources to apply their skills to other areas of involvement, such as advocacy, research, or leadership and co-ordination.

It seems that, although care and support work is important, it does not reach the attention of decision makers at the policy level because it is done on a voluntary basis. Yet it conveniently fills a gap in service provision which otherwise government policy makers would have to fill.

Lack of specific skills and knowledge

Those in power often tend to use women's lack of skills – actual, as a result of gender bias in education, training, or employment; or perceived, as an outcome of prejudice – as an excuse not to involve them in policy formulation or impact assessment. They commonly fail to recognise women's expertise and skills, and they do not attempt to support women to develop other skills through capacity-building programmes.

One of the reasons identified by ICW members for their lack of meaningful involvement was their lack of skills. *'People in government ask us, "can you formulate policies?", and we can't; we don't know where to start, how to approach people, and what questions*

to ask' (ICW workshop, Swaziland, 2005). Participants complained that when 'experts' (for example, those who determine HIV policy and programmes) had asked them, 'Do you have the skills to change policies?' and they said no, they were not taken seriously (ibid.).

Capacity building needs to be a two-way process, in which governments and businesses and organisations learn how to encourage and facilitate the meaningful involvement of women carers. One participant in our workshops commented: *'People think asking positive women to come and speak is enough. They need to be educated'* (ibid.). ICW believes that those in positions of power urgently need to build their own capacity – the capacity to engage with HIV-positive people in ways that are equitable, respectful, and productive for all involved.

Having raised some of the issues and identified the problems, in the next section I discuss some of the activities undertaken by ICW to break the deadlock.

Building bridges, confidence, and skills

At ICW, we have learned that developing advocacy skills and agendas cannot be done in a vacuum. Solidarity and support networks are vital prerequisites. ICW supports training workshops and other programmes that are designed to do the following:

- expand outreach and create self-help groups, to reduce feelings of isolation and hopelessness;

- increase the self-esteem of HIV-positive women;

- increase individual skills that strengthen networks, which will result in a wider pool of supported, knowledgeable, and effective women advocates;

- train HIV-positive women to influence public opinion, policies, and service delivery at local and national levels. This will enhance services and reduce discrimination and stigma.

ICW has been facilitating exercises that help participants to identify what needs to change in government and NGO programmes, and how and where those changes should take place. These workshops have several particularly interesting features. They are context-specific, in that they focus on the lived experience of women in a specific geographical, political, and social context; they introduce or apply gender analysis to that context; they have as an end-point an advocacy message, agenda, plan, or tool, developed by, and for use by, the participants of the workshop; and they build the capacity of workshop participants to mobilise other members of their community to engage in similar activism.

The statements by HIV-positive women quoted earlier in this article were made during an on-going project that has used this methodology to develop an advocacy-skills and advocacy-action plan in Swaziland and South Africa. This is described in the next section.

Advocacy training and development project: Swaziland and South Africa

ICW has joined forces with the POLICY project[1] and 40 HIV-positive women from Swaziland and South Africa. The agenda that has been developed focuses on asserting women's sexual and reproductive-health rights, and the right to full access to care, treatment, and support for women living with HIV/AIDS. The advocacy targets are being determined by the participants.

The project began with an assessment of the concerns and experiences of HIV-positive women in Swaziland and South Africa, and the policy and institutional environment in both countries. Information from the workshops was augmented by research and training conducted by ICW and POLICY with HIV-positive women in Swaziland.[2] This included a focus on women's access to treatment. In South Africa there has been little documentation of the experiences of HIV-positive women, so we conducted a further situation assessment with 21 women from rural and urban areas. Through this, we aimed to find out their experience within families, communities, health centres, support groups, and decision-making circles.

Women's decision-making power in sexual relationships

Women's assessment of their degrees of power in sexual relationships tended to vary, but generally they felt that they had less power than their male sexual partners to determine when and how to have sex. Comments included the following:

- 'Our partners use sex to own us.'

- 'They force us to have sex even if we don't want to.'

- 'They threaten to leave, or sleep with other women. If you refuse, the mood of the house becomes intense.'

- 'He does not force me to have sex, but he does emotionally, because if I don't, then I don't get money, he might leave or won't talk to me.'

- 'I am able to ask him to use a condom, but sometimes he refuses. That is why I stick to Femidom.'

- 'We use a male condom. It is because of our situation as a discordant couple,[3] and he never refuses.'

Caring for others when you need care yourself

Women talked of carrying the burden of caring for themselves and others: *'I was ill, and had to wake up and wash those nappies. I didn't have the strength.' ... 'We have so many challenges, and no one to take care of our health. No one to say "take your nevarapine now".'*

Community and family pressures

There was much discussion of community and family pressures on matters related to motherhood, sexuality, and sexual relations. Participants reported that family members often fail to support women's efforts to claim their sexual rights and reproductive rights. For example, in rural areas, wife inheritance is a big problem. One woman reported: *'Parents and in-laws get together to decide; the woman isn't part of the meeting, especially where* lobola *(bride-price) is paid, you are property.'*

Another said: *'My brother-in-law wanted to take my husband's place. He didn't want to marry [me, but] he wanted a sexual relationship. [He said:] "If you don't do this, we won't support the child." I told him, "Get out".'*

Disclosing one's HIV status in a difficult environment

Women agreed that theirs is a particularly difficult environment in which to disclose their status. They fear blame, violence, and abandonment. Among the women at the workshop, disclosure had occurred gradually – it was not a one-off action after a single decision. Disclosure to partners, families, friends, neighbours in the surrounding communities, and the public in general involved differing degrees of anxiety, and problems that did not necessarily diminish with time. Stigma, discrimination, and lack of support from others are common reactions when women disclose their HIV status. One commented: *'If we disclose up-front, these guys won't want to be involved. If we disclose in the middle of a relationship, we might have to start another relationship.'*

Lack of solidarity among women

Lack of solidarity among women was discussed. Most of the women felt comfortable discussing their issues with other HIV-positive women, but a number of them felt that women from beyond this group were not always supportive of them. There was lack of trust between women who were divided by other personal characteristics, including age, sexuality, socio-economic status, race, religion, and ability, and between rural and urban women. *'Women are divided – they are suspicious of each other'*, said one.

Lack of information

Lack of appropriate information for HIV-positive women on sexual and reproductive health, treatment and care, and nutrition was a concern for all: *'The information you get in health centres is government information. The basis is their programmes, so it is not necessarily on reproductive rights because that's not their stance – their stance is on how you should eat garlic.'* ... *'There is information, but it is not independent from people that are selling the [medical] products – so it is not neutral.'*

Information provided by NGOs was appreciated, but there were complaints that it is not always comprehensive enough to cover the needs of HIV-positive women, in that it tends to focus mainly on prevention.

Lack of full and appropriate health care

Women talked of the lack of appropriate, good-quality services for HIV-positive women, and the lack of cohesion between services. Family-planning advice, ante-natal services, treatment for sexually transmitted infections, and voluntary counselling and testing are offered in many but not all clinics and hospitals. This is especially the case in rural areas. Certain services are not always offered at the women's local or regular clinics.

Nearly all the women regretted the lack of services adapted to the needs and concerns of an HIV-positive woman. One woman commented: *'When I enter a clinic, I want to enter a woman's health centre where they know what to do.'* In fact, opportunities to provide comprehensive, care, treatment, and support are often missed. *'Service providers lack knowledge of proper treatment.'* ... *'When you are stressed, herpes occurs – they tell you use a condom and they don't know it's not just when you have sex.'*

There are widespread complaints about the judgemental attitudes of health-care service providers and their failure to respect confidences. Indeed, bad treatment by health-care workers was cited by the majority of women as a reason why they did not feel comfortable using official services. *'There is no confidentiality, privacy or dignity when you go to government clinics. Wherever you are, you get treated like an alien from Mars.'*

Coercion and lack of choice in reproductive-health services, testing, and treatment up-take is another major issue. One woman said: *'[If you are pregnant], they do not tell you, "if you keep it, a, b, or c is there for you" – they don't give you the option. They sterilise you. You feel obliged to take the option they offer you, or you feel you can't take the immediate service you need.'*

The participants also reported not being given preparatory and follow-up tests when seeking anti-retroviral drugs (ARVs). Hence, they were not always given the correct combination and dosage at the right time. Some women felt pressured to take ARVs when they did not feel ready. *'[The] problem goes beyond drugs – those on treatment should say that it is not just about ART, but about other treatments too. Care and support are important too.'*

Lack of meaningful involvement in policy and programme formulation

Women discussed their lack of meaningful involvement when policies and programmes were being formulated. They resented the fact that others would speak on their behalf. *'We have organisations, but men lead the organisations, and our issues don't get discussed.'*

Lack of involvement in research into prevention and treatment

It was generally felt by the women in the discussion workshops that research totally overlooked their priorities. For example, women needed microbicides, which prevent HIV transmission between sexual partners but permit women to become pregnant: *'They always focus on prevention and transmission, but what about HIV+ people that want babies? They don't bring HIV+ women to be part of the research and to say what we think about their projects, instead of deciding for us.'*

We found that there was a great deal of overlap between the experiences of the HIV-positive women from Swaziland and those of the women from South Africa. In relation to the quality of health care on offer, Swazi participants particularly complained that treatment was often not explained properly, a fact which drives away women who are seeking treatment. They reported being obliged to seek medication 'over the counter' from unqualified shop-keepers, or from traditional healers. In this situation, there is likely to be no monitoring and / or follow-up. The participants emphasised the importance of informing women about treatment and where to get it, about the medication they have been prescribed, the likely side effects, and the expected benefits.

Consolidating and prioritising the issues for advocacy

Twenty women from Swaziland and the 20 women involved in the South African assessment met in Durban in June 2005 to discuss and prioritise the issues raised in the research phase of the project. They identified the following priorities that needed to be addressed: stigma and discrimination; disclosure of HIV status; the need for access to proper care, treatment, and support; and the need for improved information on sexual and reproductive health and rights. In addition, two related areas that received particular attention were HIV testing and the criminalisation of people living with HIV and AIDS.

Testing

Currently the focus on HIV testing in many countries throughout the world, including South Africa and Swaziland, is on ante-natal testing. Although participants recognised the importance of testing pregnant women, they felt that the almost exclusive focus on testing women at ante-natal clinics meant that women were discovering their status at a very stressful time of their lives, and risked being perceived as bringing HIV into the family. Although participants welcomed more flexible opportunities for testing, they were also extremely concerned about plans to scale-up testing and to introduce a policy of routine testing.

Scaling-up testing is a cause for worry when current testing practices do not always ensure informed and voluntary consent. Some women at the workshop had heard about women being tested without any proper explanation of what they were being tested for, or even knowing whether or not they had been tested for HIV. *'I know an HIV-positive woman who was told to get tested, but she knew nothing, and then she was told she was positive. They gave her the meds without details, and she uses some meds for her kids because she does not understand.'*

Where testing is routine and supposedly voluntary, women and men may not be aware that they have the right to opt out. However, asserting that women can opt out is meaningless in a context where there is an unequal power relationship between service providers and service users. When service providers recommend women to take a test, the women often comply because the service providers are in a position of authority, and the clients may not realise that they can choose to say no. When women go home, they face pressures from family and communities concerning their sexual and reproductive lives. These may result in stigmatisation, violence, and abandonment.

Criminalisation

In South Africa, wilful transmission of HIV is a criminal offence (whether the perpetrator is a man or a woman). It is regarded as a sexual offence equivalent to rape. The women at the workshop felt strongly that HIV-negative people should bear the responsibility for protecting their own sexual health; but they also recognised that many women, particularly younger women, were not in such a position. *'Criminalisation is hard to enforce, because how do we know if a person was aware of their status? It's a law that could protect women, but where do we draw the line of confidentiality?'* Criminalisation may put pressure on people to disclose their positive status before they feel ready to do so, with consequences that might include violence, abuse, loss of livelihoods, and abandonment. Conversely, it may discourage people from getting tested.

Training and advocacy planning

The actual training and advocacy planning took place over five days in August 2005, with the same 40 women. We discussed the steps involved in advocacy, considering examples of participants' own experiences of using advocacy opportunities to achieve change in the two countries. The training workshop combined background knowledge, sharing of experiences, skills development, and planning, with the objective of producing a number of advocacy action plans that could be implemented in the coming months with continued support from ICW and POLICY Project.

The political and institutional environment

Analysing the policy and institutional environment in both countries was vital in order to ensure that participants understood the opportunities for advocacy and the constraints that compromised the chances of success.

Both Swaziland and South Africa have signed agreements that should protect the sexual and reproductive rights of HIV-positive women. These include the Convention on the Elimination of All Forms of Discrimination Against Women (CEDAW), the United Nations International Conference on Population and Development (ICPD) Platform and Programme of Action (1994), and the Windhoek Declaration (2005). This most recent agreement, signed by all the health ministers of the continent, focuses on upholding the sexual and reproductive rights of women in Africa.

Although these documents are not specific to HIV-positive women, we all share the same rights, and they can be used for leverage in advocacy initiatives. But unfortunately, the rights endorsed in these documents have yet to be reflected in national policies and programmes on HIV, AIDS, and sexually transmitted infections. Such programmes and policies continue to ignore the rights of HIV-positive women. This is no doubt a direct result of the women's lack of involvement in decision making, as described above. Governments' lack of consideration for the rights of HIV-positive women was demonstrated all too harshly at our workshop: the government representative who had been invited to give a presentation (and who had confirmed an intention to attend) failed to attend the event, without bothering even to offer an excuse.

There is, however, some movement for change. Swaziland does have a draft policy on gender equality – although it has been in draft form since 2000. The Swazi government is also developing a policy and strategy on reproductive health, with input from POLICY and ICW. South Africa, on the other hand, is developing a bill on equity in marriage, and care and confidentiality in the health sector.

Although they are not sufficiently specific for HIV-positive women, these draft laws and policies do provide advocacy opportunities for our members. During the workshop we examined these policy documents. ICW had been invited by those drafting the policies to give feedback on them, with provision for participants' comments to be fed directly into current efforts to influence policy makers. For example, one of the articles in the Equity in Marriage Bill states that couples should be tested for HIV before they are married, and the women at the workshop were alarmed about the possible fate of a woman if she tested positive at this stage.

Examples of advocacy work

Some of the participants were invited to share examples of advocacy from their own personal experience, and this was used as a basis for identifying the various components of the advocacy process. Two examples of advocacy cited by our participants are included here.

On hearing that the Swazi army refused to recruit people living with HIV, one of the participants had tried to join up in order to raise people's awareness of this discrimination. She was paraded naked in front of a male doctor, then told she could not join because she had keloids (scar tissue), and her 'blood was bad'. The ICW Southern African Co-ordinator is working with women in Swaziland to try to get this discriminatory regulation overturned.

A number of activists in South Africa have recently formed a coalition called Womandla, which aims to ensure that the voices of HIV-positive women are heard in national responses to HIV. One of their first objectives was to attend a recent national AIDS conference in Durban. However, the registration fee was greater than the cost of six months' worth of anti-retroviral drug treatment. They picketed at the conference, and were eventually able to secure entry for three of their number.

Examples of advocacy work were also given by external presenters from the Treatment Action Campaign (RSA), the Reproductive Health Alliance (RSA), and Women In Law In Southern Africa (Swaziland). They helped us to understand advocacy strategies used by other organisations, and they formed part of an important and on-going process of building alliances. This programme is supported by a reference group consisting of women from a number of key organisations working on women's rights and HIV, who offered their support in the development and implementation of advocacy strategies.

Developing advocacy plans

The following advocacy goals were chosen, and plans were developed accordingly.

Goal: To make available alternative technologies which prevent the transmission of HIV while allowing conception. **How?** By demanding that government should incorporate appropriate measures into already existing family-planning programmes.

Goal: to guarantee the sexual and reproductive rights of HIV-positive women, including the right to good-quality services. **How?** By urging the Ministry of Health to provide in all regional hospitals by 2010 annual pap smears for HIV-positive women, and free monitoring tests such as CD4 counts and viral load services, and breast-cancer services.

Goal: to involve HIV-positive women – in an ethical manner – in research. **How?** Initially by promoting existing methodologies that effectively incorporate a gender-equality approach in academic institutions and among researchers.

Goal: to ensure that the rights of HIV-positive women in rural and urban areas are protected in their homes and communities. **How?** By demanding the development of a policy that protects and enforces the property rights of all HIV-positive women (by December 2006).

Goal: to enable HIV-positive women to adopt children. **How?** By calling on Swaziland's government to develop an adoption policy by December 2008 to allow HIV-positive women to adopt children freely.

Goal: care and support for HIV-positive women in their communities. **How?** By building the capacity of 200 HIV-positive women in their communities so that by June 2006 they have knowledge of the health services that are currently offered to 50 women in each region of Swaziland, through health centres and government hospitals.

We now have seven exciting advocacy-action plans which the forty participants, with support from ICW staff, will aim to implement over the coming months. There are many obstacles ahead, but with combined strength we hope to ensure better polices and programmes for HIV-positive women and their families and communities. (It is hoped to report on the progress of these plans in future News Sections of *Gender and Development.*)

To conclude this article, one of the participants reflects on the workshop and the challenges facing HIV-positive women activists in implementing their plans:

'On my side a big gap was covered in the August workshop. Gaining skills was the main goal I wanted to achieve in this workshop. We were able to put down our action plans, which we hope will be implemented. I learned how to be an active advocate, how other people have advocated for something before. Knowing the outcomes of their actions helps to find an effective way of advocating. I learned how to put down strategies and smart objectives.

'We face a big problem when challenging our enemies. The problem might be that the person who is an enemy to us is the very person who is supposed to fall under our allies' list, e.g men are against condoms yet they should protect themselves, the next thing they blame a lady for bringing such disease at home. Another challenge is funding. It is very hard to get a kick start for funding. A further challenge at the time of writing in Swaziland is that it is impossible to find a complete policy document. Almost all the copies of policies that we have to use to inform our advocacy work are drafts, which makes it hard to implement. We also do not have individual champions who are HIV-positive women in high positions to help us push for the implementation.

'Another challenge is that people still believe that if you are HIV-positive you [are] suppose[d] to be sick or having oppor-tunistic infections or… a sign which shows that you are positive. If a person like me is advocating for such issues, they just say that I am lying, I do that because I am given some money, meaning that I was bribed. For example, when I was exhibiting at the trade fair,[4] people would just come now and then, thinking that I will change my story. For example someone came twice and more, saying "Anya, come on now, the game is over, I would really like to know if you are a lady living with HIV or you just making a joke with it. I have been thinking about it over-night, you just want us to test, and what I can tell you is that you know nothing about issues for HIV-positive people, you don't know what they go through, so get a life". Man, it's surprising because these people are just like me. What I can say is that it takes an arm and a leg to be an advocate, but I am really proud of carrying out such work, as I know that not only allies will benefit from that but also enemies.'

Emma Bell works for the International Community of Women Living with HIV/AIDS. Address: Unit 6, Building 1, Canonbury Yard, 190a New North Road, London N1 7BJ. If you would like further information about the work of the ICW, please contact Emma Bell at emma@icw.org.

Notes

1 The POLICY Project endeavours to improve policies affecting family planning, reproductive health, HIV/AIDS, and maternal health programmes and services in developing countries. Multi-sectoral collaboration, community empowerment, respect for human rights and gender equality, and support for vulnerable populations, including orphans and other children affected by HIV/AIDS, characterise POLICY's approach to policy and programme development.

2 In October 2004, ICW ran an advocacy training workshop with 20 HIV-positive young women from Swaziland, and in February 2005 another workshop with 20 HIV-positive women, with the aim of monitoring government commitment to the rights of HIV-positive women. A similar workshop was held in Lesotho.

3 A 'discordant couple' is a couple in a sexual relationship in which one person is HIV-negative and the other is HIV-positive.

4 The trade fair is an event that occurs yearly in Swaziland in the summer. ICW has run a stand there, together with SWAPOL (Swaziland Positive Living).

Resources

Compiled by Kanika Lang

Publications

Globalizing Women: Transnational Feminist Networks (2005)
Valentine M. Moghadam
Johns Hopkins University Press, 2715 N. Charles Street, Baltimore, Maryland 21218-4319, USA
www.press.jhu.edu

This book explores the theme of transnational feminist networks and their relationship to globalisation. The author examines how women are responding to the negative consequences of economic and cultural globalisation – and to the rise of religious fundamentalism in particular. Global feminist networks are able to use globalised communications methods for their advocacy and lobbying. The book focuses on three feminist networks formed in opposition to structural adjustment and neo-liberal economic policy, and three networks that promote women's human rights, especially in Muslim countries.

Feminist Politics, Activism and Vision: Local and Global Challenges (2004)
Luciana Ricciutelli, Angela Miles, and Margaret H. McFadden (eds.)
Zed Books, 7 Cynthia Street, London N1 9JF, UK
www.zedbooks.co.uk

This rich collection presents stimulating and insightful analyses of the challenges facing feminists in the world today, as well as accounts of strategies that they have employed at local, national, regional and transnational levels, in the face of these challenges. In each of its five parts, academic-activist authors draw on their own experience and analysis of feminist activities in countries and regions of the world, including Singapore, the Niger Delta, India, Latin America, the USA, and Africa. Part 1 provides feminist analyses of the economic context of current global and local feminist activism. Part 2 analyses national, regional, and transnational feminist advocacy efforts – their challenges and responses. Part 3 provides concrete examples of women's struggles in communities around the world, and their links to feminist networks and analyses. Part 4 discusses questions about the sources of and challenges to feminism's transformative power. Part 5 summarises some of the main arguments that run through the different articles.

The Future of Women's Rights: Global Visions and Strategies (2004)
Joanna Kerr, Ellen Sprenger, and Alison Symington (eds.)
Zed Books, 7 Cynthia Street, London N1 9JF, UK
www.zedbooks.co.uk

This book emerged from a collaborative project between the Association for

Women's Rights in Development (AWID) and Mama Cash. Representing a diverse collection of views and positions, contributors address two main questions: what are the emerging trends and developments that will have an impact on women's rights? and what are the best strategies to respond to these trends? They discuss the current backlash against women and attacks on their human rights which are the outcome of unequal global economic systems, increased militarisation and religious extremism, and the HIV/AIDS pandemic. Proposed strategies to deal with these challenges include strengthening women's, and feminist, movements and alliances, supporting strong women's grassroots organisations, strengthening local and global links, and pressuring governments to ensure equal political participation.

Developing Power: How Women Transformed International Development (2004)
Arvonne S. Fraser and Irene Tinker (eds.)
The Feminist Press, City University of New York, The Graduate Center, 365 Fifth Avenue, Suite 5406, New York, NY 10016, USA,
www.feministpress.org

This is a collection of personal testimonies by 27 women who were pioneers in the global women's movement. Each story provides fascinating insights into the personal lives and motivations of these women, as well as documenting key events and processes in the struggle to gain equality for women over the past four decades. Writers include Irene Tinker, Margaret Snyder, Peggy Antrobus, and Kathleen Staudt.

The Global Women's Movement: Origins, Issues and Strategies (2004)
Peggy Antrobus
Zed Books, 7 Cynthia Street, London N1 9JF, UK
www.zedbooks.co.uk

Written by one of the founding members of DAWN (Development Alternatives with Women for a New Era), this book traces the development of the global women's movement. It analyses the movement's origins in local movements mobilised around issues of citizenship, rights, and participation, and provides an overview of the history of women's organising and collective action from the 1960s onwards. Interspersing personal reflections from a key participant in the events described, the author discusses current challenges faced and possible strategies for the future of the movement.

Common Ground or Mutual Exclusion? Women's Movements and International Relations (2002)
Marianne Braig and Sonja Wolte
Zed Books, 7 Cynthia Street, London N1 9JF, UK
www.zedbooks.co.uk

This collection of articles examines the influence of women's movements in three policy areas: development policy/studies; women's human rights; and peace and conflict resolution. In doing so, the authors emphasise certain common themes. They agree that the women's movement cannot be conceptualised as homogeneous: it is a coalition of diverse social movements of women who differ from each other by virtue of class, ethnicity, and other factors. Other major themes running through the book are the importance of the relationship between feminist politics and feminist scholarship, and the question of whether it is possible to lobby, exert influence, and seek inclusion in mainstream politics while retaining the radical edge of women's political activism.

Primers from AWID
available online at
www.awid.org/publications/primers

This resource from AWID is useful for feminist advocates working at national, regional, and transnational levels. Primers focus on the Convention on the Elimination of All Forms of Discrimination Against Women (CEDAW); Women's Human Rights; Intersectionality; New Reproductive Technologies; Challenging Neoliberal Globalisation; Women's Rights and the World Trade Organisation; and International Trade Policy. Spanish and French versions of many of these primers are included on the same website.

Addressing Financial Stability: Key Challenges and Opportunities for Transnational Women's Rights Organizations (2002) AWID
Available online at:
www.awid.org/publications/occasional 10.doc

This paper is the result of a study initiated by the Association for Women's Rights in Development (AWID). It discusses sources of current funding for international women's organisations, and the strategies that these organisations use to secure funds. The authors also scan the environment for potential new sources of funding over the next two to five years, exploring how donors might be more motivated to support transnational women's organisations, and the kinds of message or information that would help to clarify the vital role that they play.

Leading to Choices: A Leadership Training Handbook for Women (2001)
Mahnaz Afkhami, Ann Eisenberg, and Haleh Vaziri
Women's Learning Partnership for Rights, Development, and Peace, 4343 Montgomery Avenue, Suite 201, Bethesda, MD 20814, USA
www.learningpartnership.org
Available online at:
http://learningpartnership.org/publications/ltcpdfs/engltcmanual.pdf (Also available in other languages from the WLP website)

Leading to Choices is a training manual focusing on leadership styles used by feminists. It features a contextual chapter, 12 workshop sessions, and an appendix containing culture-specific scenarios to cultivate effective leadership skills.

Global Feminisms Since 1945 (2000)
Bonnie G. Smith (ed.)
Routledge, Taylor & Francis Group
2 Park Square, Milton Park, Abingdon, Oxford OX14 4RN, UK
www.routledge.com

Authors in this collection tell the story of women's activism for equality, liberation, and better lives from 1945 onwards. The book is divided into four parts. The first documents feminisms in the context of nation-building efforts in Egypt, Vietnam, and South Africa; the second discusses activism in Brazil, Kenya, and South Korea; the third details the women's liberation movement in the USA, Britain, and Japan; and the fourth discusses the new wave of feminism in the 1980s and 1990s, in post-Soviet Russia, Iran, and Germany.

Missionaries and Mandarins: Feminist engagements with development institutions (1998)
Carol Miller and Shahra Razavi (eds.)
ITDG Publishing, Intermediate Technology Development Group, Bourton Hall, Bourton-on-Dunsmore, Rugby, CV23 9QZ UK
www.developmentbookshop.com

The articles in this book describe the strategies of – and challenges for – feminists working within development institutions (including state bureaucracies, multilateral organisations, and NGOs). Various feminist strategies are presented, together with case studies from New Zealand, Australia, Canada, Vietnam, Uganda, Chile, and Morocco. The importance of the relationship between 'insiders' (feminists working within development organisations), and 'outsiders' (feminists working in organised women's movements) in transforming development organisations is a central theme of many of the articles.

Women's Human Rights Step by Step: Practical Guide to Using International Human Rights Law and Mechanisms to Defend Women's Human Rights (1997)
Human Rights Watch Women's Rights Project

This is a book about women's human rights in practice. It describes the concept and content of human-rights law and its application to women and to the rights issues that concern them particularly. Designed as a basic guide to the operation of human-rights mechanisms and the strategies at national, regional, and international levels, the manual explains how to use these strategies and mechanisms to uphold women's human rights. It offers a wide range of possible strategies to consider in defending the human rights of women.

Integrative Feminisms: Building Global Visions, 1960s-1990s (1996)
Angela Miles
Routledge, Taylor & Francis 2 Park Square, Milton Park, Abingdon, Oxford OX14 4RN, UK
www.routledge.com

Written by a Canadian feminist, this book presents a theoretical analysis of the politics of feminist radicalism in a global context. The author focuses on what she terms 'integrative feminist politics' – that is, the shared values and visions of feminists located in North America and the global South. She argues that types of feminism that are usually perceived as absolutely different, even opposing, have important principles in common.

The Challenge of Local Feminisms: Women's Movements in Global Perspective (1995)
Amrita Basu (ed.)
Westview Press, HarperCollins International, Export Department, 10 East 53rd Street, New York, NY 10022, USA
www.westviewpress.com

This collection of articles aims to introduce readers to women's movements beyond those in the USA and Western Europe, focusing on post-colonial nations of Asia, Africa, and Latin America. Authors discuss examples of movements fronted by both middle-class and poor women; the importance of the extent to which these movements are grounded in local realities; and the importance of the link between local and global women's movements, ensuring that feminists can interact, exchange ideas, and learn from each other.

Women for Change: A Grassroots Guide to Activism and Politics (1995)
Thalia Zepatos and Elizabeth Kaufman
Facts on File, Inc, 460 Park Avenue South,
New York, NY 10016

Although written as a guide for activism in the USA, this book provides insights into strategies and tools that have uses beyond the US. With advice for women on how to form a group to fight for power, the authors outline the skills needed for leadership. They also explain how political campaigns work, with the intention of encouraging more women to become actively involved in political action.

Electronic resources

Women's Human Rights Net:
www.whrnet.org

WHRnet aims to provide reliable, comprehensive, and timely information and analyses on women's human rights in English, Spanish, and French. WHRnet updates readers on women's human-rights issues and policy developments globally and provides information and analyses that support advocacy actions. A team of regionally based content specialists provides regular News, Interviews, Perspectives, Alert and Campaign information, and Web Highlights. The site provides an introduction to women's human-rights issues worldwide; an overview of UN/Regional Human Rights Systems; a Research Tool that serves as a gateway to the best available online resources relevant to advocacy for women's human rights; and a comprehensive collection of related Links.

Women's Human Rights Resources (WHRR):
www.law-lib.utoronto.ca/Diana/

WHRR is a free online library of international women's-rights law. The purpose is to help researchers, students, teachers, and human-rights advocates to obtain authoritative and diverse information on women's international human rights via the Internet. It includes a searchable database, advocacy guides, and legal research guides on international women's rights law.

Global Feminist Activism in Focus (2004)
Women in Action, Isis:
www.isiswomen.org/pub/wia/wia2-04/editorial.htm

This issue of the newsletter *Women in Action* by Isis International brings together the perspectives, reflections, and ruminations of feminist activists on the changing nature of the women's movement and feminist strategies, in the context of a terrain vastly different from that in which they began more than three decades ago. Some contributors express doubts about feminist global-level strategies. Others stress the need for women at the grassroots to be involved in transnational events like the World Conference on Women. Dilemmas implied by the need to work closely with the State are examined, as is the notion of gender mainstreaming. The issue also contains a dialogue among feminists on the shifts in the women's movement, its strategies and relationship to other social-justice movements. Contributors include Peggy Antrobus, Ewa Charkiewicz, Suzette Mitchell, and Sunila Abeysekera.

Stop Violence Against Women (STOPVAW): www.stopvaw.org

This website is a forum for information, advocacy, and change, developed as a tool for the promotion of women's human rights in the countries of Central and Eastern Europe (CEE) and the Commonwealth of Independent States (CIS), Mongolia, and the UN Protectorate of Kosovo. This site addresses violence against women as one of the most pervasive abuses of human rights worldwide. STOPVAW provides women's-rights advocates with information and advocacy tools to end the most endemic forms of violence against women in the region: domestic violence; sexual assault; sexual harassment; and trafficking in women.

Developing an Advocacy Strategy (on STOPVAW website)
www.stopvaw.org/Developing_an_Advocacy_Strategy.html

Although it is located on the Violence Against Women section of UNIFEM's website, this brief guide, adapted in part from *Women's Human Rights Step by Step*, can be used more widely by advocates in developing an advocacy strategy on women's rights issues. It discusses nine steps involved in developing an advocacy strategy.

Feminist.com: www.feminist.com/

Feminist.com is an activist community and portal of resources and information that supports women's equality, justice, wellness, and safety. The website was founded to initiate and facilitate grassroots mobilisation, networking, and communication on important political, health, and educational issues related to women. Feminist.com supports women-friendly organisations and citizen participation, promotes women's business development, and encourages women's self-sufficiency.

The website is a interactive on-line community which offers resources for all women and provides a safe space for diverse dialogues.

Resource for Activist Websites for Women's Issues
http://research.umbc.edu/~korenman/wmst/links_actv.html

A collection of links to websites on activism on women's issues.

Women in Sync: Toolkit for Electronic Networking
www.apcwomen.org/netsupport/sync/sync.html

The Women's Networking Support Programme (WNSP) is a global network of women who support women working for social change and women's empowerment, through the use of Information and Communication Technologies (ICTs). The website 'Women in Sync' hosts a collection of stories about the experiences of the women and their organisations who have become a part of the WNSP's network. The website provides a toolkit for women's electronic networking. The Toolkit comes in three parts. The first presents feedback from the 40 women who worked on the APC communications Project in Beijing during the 4th World Conference on Women in 1995.The second kit examines the growth of the APCWNSP from a small group of women, to a programme that has spawned global networking initiatives. The third kit is a collection of women's networking experiences from Africa, Asia, Latin America, and Europe.

Advocacy on Women's Issues
www.cld.org/wipdbfadv.htm

Hosted by The Centre for Legislative Development, Philippines, this website offers an assortment of resources on women's issues, including engagement with the Beijing Platform for Action, information on advocacy manuals, and case studies from around the world on women's rights advocacy.

Organisations

Development Alternatives With Women For A New Era (DAWN)
www.dawn.org.fj

DAWN is a network of women scholars and activists from the economic South who engage in feminist research and analysis of the global environment and are committed to working for economic justice, gender justice, and democracy. DAWN works globally and regionally in Africa, Asia, the Caribbean, Latin America, and the Pacific on the themes of the Political Economy of Globalisation; Political Restructuring and Social Transformation; Sustainable Livelihoods; and Sexual and Reproductive Health and Rights, in partnership with other global NGOs and networks.

The Association for Women's Rights in Development (AWID)
Toronto Secretariat: 215 Spadina Ave., Suite 150, Toronto, Ontario, M5T 2C7, Canada
www.awid.org; awid@awid.org

AWID is an international membership organisation connecting, informing, and mobilising people and organisations committed to achieving gender equality, sustainable development, and women's human rights. Its goal is to cause policy, institutional, and individual change that will improve the lives of women and girls everywhere, and do this by facilitating ongoing debates on fundamental and provocative issues, as well as by building the individual and organisational capacities of those working for women's empowerment and social justice.

Women's International Coalition for Economic Justice (WICEJ)
12 Dongan Place #206, New York, NY 10040, USA
www.wicej.org; info@wicej.org

WICEJ is an international coalition representing organisations in all regions of the globe. It works to link gender with macro-economic policy in international inter-government policy-making arenas, from a human-rights perspective. WICEJ uses an integrated feminist analysis which links the multiplicity of systems that oppress women, and recognises the diversity of women's experience by race, ethnicity, class, national origin, citizenship status, and other factors. It seeks to bring local perspectives on gender and economic issues to the international arena, and to communicate shared analysis from the international arena back to regions and national communities.

Women's Environment & Development Organization (WEDO)
355 Lexington Avenue, 3rd Floor, New York, NY 10017-6603, USA
wedo@wedo.org; www.wedo.org

Established in 1990, WEDO is an international advocacy network which seeks to increase the power of women worldwide as policy makers in governance and in policy-making institutions, forums and processes, at all levels, to achieve economic and social justice, a peaceful and healthy planet, and human rights for all. WEDO's programme areas are Gender and Governance, Sustainable Development, and Economic and Social Justice. WEDO campaigns for women's equality in economic and political decision making, seeks development solutions that are sustainable for women, communities, and the planet, promotes economic equity for women, and increases public awareness about the negative impacts of globalisation on women, their families and their communities, and the environment.

Women's Learning Partnership for Rights, Development, and Peace (WLP)
4343 Montgomery Avenue, Suite 201, Bethesda, MD 20814, USA
wlp@learningpartnership.org
www.learningpartnership.org

WLP empowers women and girls in the Global South to re-imagine and re-structure their roles in their families, communities, and societies. WLP achieves this goal through providing leadership training, supporting capacity building, and helping women to use new technologies to generate and receive information and knowledge. WLP conducts all of its work in collaboration with partner organisations located in Africa, Asia, and the Middle East, and with members of an international network of experts.

The African Women's Development Fund (AWDF)
25 Yiyiwa St. Achimota Forest, Ablenkpe, Accra, Ghana, PMB CT89 Cantonments, Accra, Ghana
www.awdf.org; awdf@awdf.org

AWDF, established in June 2000, is the first Africa-wide fund-raising and grant-making fund. It funds local, national, sub-regional, and regional organisations in Africa working towards women's empowerment. The objectives are fund-raising within and outside Africa, grant making on an Africa-wide basis, communicating the work and achievements of African women's organisations, and providing technical assistance to grantees.

The Gender Advocacy Programme (GAP)
7 Ruskin House, 2 Roeland Street, Cape Town, 8001, South Africa
reception@gender.org.za
www.gender.co.za

The Gender Advocacy Programme (GAP) is an independent, non-government advocacy and lobbying organisation based in Cape Town. Its aim is to bridge the gap between women in civil society and structures of governance, and to increase the participation of women in policy formulation and decision making. GAP conducts research and training to facilitate, mobilise, link, and empower women to lobby for equity between men and women in all spheres of South African society. GAP has adopted the role of 'policy midwife', by translating the legal jargon of legislation into accessible language so that marginalised women can advocate and lobby for themselves.

Isis International
Isis International Manila: 3 Marunong St., Barangay Central, Quezon City, Philippines 1100
www.isiswomen.org; admin@isiswomen.org
Isis International Chile: www.isis.cl, isis@isis.cl
Isis International Uganda: Isis-Women's International Cross Cultural Exchange (Isis-WICCE), Plot 32 Bukoto Street – Kamwokya, PO BOX 4934, Kampala, Uganda,
www.isis.or.ug/, isis@starcom.co.ug

Isis International is a feminist NGO dedicated to women's information and communication needs. It focuses on advancing women's rights, leadership, and empowerment in Asia and the Pacific. With connections in more than 150 countries, it keeps up with changing trends and analyses concerning women worldwide. Isis International has three independent offices in Asia (Manila, Philippines), Africa (Kampala, Uganda), and Latin America (Santiago, Chile), reflecting a commitment to South–South cooperation and South–North linkages.

The Center for Women's Global Leadership (Global Center)
Douglass College, Rutgers, The State University of New Jersey, 160 Ryders Lane, New Brunswick, NJ 08901-8555 USA
cwgl@igc.org; www.cwgl.rutgers.edu

The Global Center develops and facilitates women's leadership for women's human rights and social justice worldwide. It is a unit of the Institute for Women's Leadership (IWL)—a consortium of six women's programmes at Rutgers University. The Global Center's programmes promote the leadership of women and advance feminist perspectives in policy-making processes in local, national, and international arenas. Since 1990, the Global Center has fostered women's leadership in the area of human rights through women's global leadership institutes, strategic planning activities, international mobilisation campaigns, UN monitoring, global education endeavours, publications, and a resource centre. The Global Center works from a human-rights perspective with an emphasis on preventing violence against women, and promoting sexual and reproductive health and socio-economic well being. The Global Center's programmes are in two broad areas: policy and advocacy, and leadership development and women's human-rights education.

Global Women's Strike
Crossroads Women's Centre, 230a Kentish Town Road, London NW5 2AB, UK
womenstrike8m@server101.com; www.globalwomenstrike.net

The Global Women's Strike was born in 1999, when women in Ireland decided to welcome the new millennium with a national general strike. Since then, they have been campaigning for recognition and wages for all the unwaged work that women do, as well as for pay equity. Since 2000, the Strike has brought together women in more than 60 countries, including grassroots organisations which demand a world that values all women's work and life. They are now part of an international network of Strike co-ordinators. International co-ordination is done in England by the Crossroads Women's Centre. Details of other groups are on the website given above.

Womankind Worldwide
32–37, 2nd Floor, Development House, 56-64 Leonard Street, London EC2A 4JX, UK
www.womankind.org.uk; info@womankind.org.uk

Womankind Worldwide is a UK-based charity dedicated to women's development and women's human rights globally. Womankind has developed programmes in partnership with local community groups, to tackle women's inequality in many of the world's poorest places. These programmes are called the Four Literacies: Word Literacy, Money Literacy, Body Literacy, and Civil Literacy. They aim to unlock women's potential and maximise their ability to make decisions in their own lives, the lives of their family, as well as in the future of their community and country. Womankind works with 70 partner organisations in 20 countries, spanning Africa, South Asia, Central and South America, and Europe.

Women In Development Europe (WIDE)
rue de la Science 10, 1000 Brussels, Belgium
www.eurosur.org/wide/home.htm; info@wide-network.org

WIDE is a European network of development NGOs, gender specialists, and human-rights activists. It monitors and influences international economic and development policy and practice from a feminist perspective. WIDE's work is grounded in women's rights as the basis for the development of a more just and democratic world order. WIDE strives for a world based on gender equality and social justice which ensures equal rights for all, as well as equal access to resources and opportunities in all spheres of political, social, and economic life.

Women Living Under Muslim Laws (WLUML)
Africa & Middle East Coordination Office: BAOBAB for Women's Human Rights, PO Box 73630, Victoria Island, Lagos, Nigeria; baobab@baobabwomen.org   ; www.baobabwomen.org
Asia Coordination Office: Shirkat Gah Women's Resource Centre, PO Box 5192, Lahore, Pakistan; sgah@sgah.org.pk
International Coordination Office: PO Box 28445, London, N19 5NZ, UK; wluml@wluml.org

WLUML is an international solidarity network which provides information, support, and a collective space for women whose lives are shaped, conditioned, or governed by laws and customs said to derive from Islam. It now extends to more than 70 countries, ranging from South Africa to Uzbekistan, Senegal to Indonesia, and Brazil to France. WLUML's current focus is on the themes of fundamentalisms and militarisation, and their impact on women's lives, and sexuality. As a theme, violence against women cuts across all of WLUML's projects and activities. Using a variety of media, it responds to, circulates, and initiates international alerts for action and campaigns, as requested by net-working groups and allies. It also provides concrete support for individual women in the form of information on their legal rights, assistance with asylum applications, links with relevant support institutions, and psychological support. WLUML puts women in direct contact with each other to facilitate a non-hierarchical exchange of information, expertise, strategies and experience. It builds the capacity of networking groups through internships and exchanges at the co-ordination offices, and training and workshops.

Research Action and Information Network for the Bodily Integrity of Women (RAINBO)
Suite 5A, Queens Studios, 121 Salisbury Road, London NW6 6RG
info@rainbo.org ; www.rainbo.org

RAINBO is an African-led international NGO working on issues of women's empowerment, gender, reproductive health, sexual autonomy, and freedom from violence as central components of the African development agenda. The work of RAINBO is divided into two main programmatic areas: Integrated Initiative Against FGM, including the Small Grants Project; and AMANITARE, the African Partnership for the Sexual and Reproductive Health & Rights of Women and Girls.

Fawcett Society
1-3 Berry Street, London, EC1V 0AA, UK
w w w . f a w c e t t s o c i e t y . o r g . u k ; info@fawcettsociety.org.uk

Fawcett Society campaigns for equality between women and men. It examines laws and policy proposals in terms of their impact on women and publicises the results to politicians, the media, women's organisations, and individual women. It commissions and conducts research into gender inequalities and produces campaign packs for members and the public, to enable them to raise issues themselves.

Equality Now
www.equalitynow.org
New York office: PO Box 20646, Columbus Circle Station, New York, NY 10023, USA, info@equalitynow.org
Africa Regional office: PO Box 2018 KNH 00202, Nairobi, Kenya, equalitynow@kenyaweb.com
London office: PO Box 48822, London WC2N 6ZW, UK, ukinfo@equalitynow.org

Equality Now was founded in 1992 to work for the protection and promotion of the human rights of women around the world. Working with national human-rights organisations and individual activists, Equality Now documents violence and discrimination against women and mobilises international action to support their efforts to stop these abuses. Through its Women's Action Network, which links concerned groups and individuals around the world, Equality Now distributes information about human-rights violations, takes action to protest against these violations, and draws public attention to the violations of women's human rights.

The Network of East–West Women (NEWW)
Stowarzyszenie Wspólpracy Kobiet, Neww-Polska, ul. Miszewskiego 17 p. 100, 80 - 239 GDAŇSK
www.neww.org ; neww@neww.org.pl

Founded in 1991, NEWW is an international communication and resource network supporting dialogue, information exchange, and activism among those concerned about the status of women in Central and Eastern Europe, the Newly Independent States, and the Russian Federation. NEWW co-ordinates research and advocacy that supports women's equality and full participation in all aspects of public and private life. NEWW connects women's advocates who work in partnership to promote women's rights and to strengthen women's role within civil society. NEWW's overarching goal is to support the formation of independent women's movements and to strengthen the capacities of women and women's NGOs to influence policy regarding women's lives.

Feminist Majority Foundation
1600 Wilson Boulevard, Suite 801, Arlington, VA 22209, USA, and 433 S. Beverly Drive, Beverly Hills, CA 90212, USA
www.feminist.org

The Feminist Majority Foundation (FMF) is an organisation dedicated to women's equality, reproductive health, and non-violence. In all spheres, FMF utilises research and action to empower women economically, socially, and politically. FMF's research and action programmes focus on advancing the legal, social, and political equality of women with men, countering the backlash to women's advancement, and recruiting and training young feminists to encourage future leadership for the feminist movement in the United States. To carry out these aims, FMF engages in research and public policy development, public education programmes, grassroots organising projects, leadership training and development programmes, and participates in and organises forums on issues of women's equality and empowerment.